Protecting the Human Resource:
The HR Guide to Ergonomics
Naomi Abrams, OTD, OTR/L, CEAS

NAOE Publishing

Published by NAOE Publications
Rockville, Maryland
Copyright © 2017 Naomi Abrams

ISBN: 978-0-9839582-1-5

Special thanks to Susan Shaw for helping with the appendices,
and Fran Abrams (aka Mom) and Bethany Portner for jumping in with grammar help.

Table of Contents

Introduction

Over the years, I have received many questions from human resource professionals. Here are some examples:

"What is ergonomics?"

"What do you think about {fill in the blank} equipment?"

"Which chair should I buy?"

"Why did I never know there was someone out there who could help me with this?"

"Is the expense worth it?"

I wrote this book in response to these questions, and many more, in the hope of providing HR professionals with a go-to resource to understand ergonomics, a field of science that I am passionate about. Humans are the greatest resource companies have and are integral to every company around the world. After years of treating injured workers as an occupational therapist, I changed my career direction to focus on preventing injuries before they happen. By the time people ended up in my clinic, their lives had been disrupted, their workplaces challenged, and resources strained. My motto: Prevention is the least expensive cure.

This book will teach you how to better recognize problem areas so that you can prevent workplace injuries, both acute and repetitive, that ultimately cost your company. The purpose of this book is not to teach you to be an ergonomist, but how to identify problems and then ensure that the solution presented by the experts will be effective.

Using This Book

This book is divided into four parts: what, why, how, and who (and a few bonus resources).

I also have added sections specific to different ergonomics concerns and programming for the office and for industrial settings.

In each section, I strive to give you information to be a savvy shopper of ergonomics programs. The only way to know what to do is to know what you don't know and where you want to go. We will discuss what fits into your goals and your budgets. Warning: some of the exercises and challenges will take some research on your part—don't skip ahead.

Ergonomics requires an investment of your employees, management, facilities, and engineers—it doesn't have to be hard, but you do need to have a good idea of your employee's current state of health, program participation, and injury. Your employees are your greatest resource; they are what keeps your company going. Use this book for how it was meant: to protect them and help them work efficiently and without injury. Yup, you will save a boatload of money in the end, but I want to be sure all of this saving money is prefaced by an understanding that you will be most successful if you come at ergonomics programming with the plan to protect and help your employees.

Before you dive in—your challenge: Understand your preconceived notions, why you bothered to read this book, where this issue hits your company, and what your company will buy into.

Answer the following

What are your three greatest concerns about ergonomics programming?

What do you think of when you think "ergonomics?"

Where have you spent the most money so far on ergonomics (equipment, training, lost time)?

How does ergonomics fit into your company's goals?

Part I: What is Ergonomics?

Chapter 1: Ergonomics: True Injury Prevention

Ergonomics Defined

In easy-to-understand terms, ergonomics is the science that studies whether and how a human can do a job without breaking something (their own body or the thing they are producing). In more complex terms, the International Ergonomics Association (2000) defined ergonomics as:

> *"The scientific discipline concerned with the understanding of the interactions among humans and other elements of a system, and the profession that applies theoretical principles, data and methods to design in order to optimize human wellbeing and overall system* [1]*"*

An ergonomics evaluation is used to better understand the complex interactions of the components of work: the person, the tools used, and the environmental contexts. Ergonomics simply provides a scientific method and a language for studying the capabilities of humans in relationship to the requirements of the job (such as back compression studies or force lifting measures).

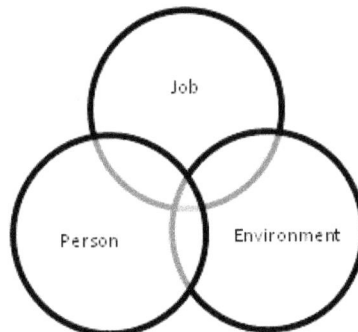

There are three acceptable uses for the term ergonomic(s): the name for a field of study – ergonomics, the description of the people who study in this field, such as ergonomics experts or ergonomists, and the type of program or assessment, such as an ergonomics program or ergonomics assessment. The use of the term "ergonomic" with consumer products has little to no validity. Stamping a product, such as chair or drill, with the word "ergonomic" is a marketing affectation to entice purchasers to pay more for a product. For a product to be measured as having few ergonomics risk factors it would need to fit a specific task, person, and environment. It is impossible for one product to be risk free for all populations in all situations and therefore worthy of the title "ergonomic." For the field of ergonomics, the result of the risks or "problem" most often studied is what happens when the work task exceeds the person's abilities (physical, psychological, or mental), also known as **injury**.

Understanding Injuries

Most people don't wake up and say, "Today I am going to do something really stupid and hurt myself." However, there are plenty of people who repeatedly do things that cause them pain and then wonder afterward why they hurt so much. There are two broad classifications of injury for our purposes: acute and repetitive strain (RSI).

Acute injury is the type we are all fairly good at recognizing. If something starts to bleed profusely, or hurts a whole lot because we smashed it, or if we suddenly find ourselves on the floor when we used to be standing up, we are fairly sure that something has gone wrong. These acute injuries usually don't have any advance warning. We just deal with them as they come.

Repetitive strain injuries are often called work-related musculoskeletal disorders (WRMSDs)—although this is a bit of a misnomer since WRMSDs also can occur with acute injury or because of strains to the body that did not occur at work. RSI/WRMSDs have a multifactorial nature that makes finding the cause of the injury difficult. As a result, the study of the causes of those injuries often becomes controversial and can degenerate into a blame game fought in workers' compensation courts.[2] Repetitive strains are injuries that occur from repeated use of one or more body structures. The injuries that fall under this classification are related to muscles, tendons, nerves, bones, and ligaments. There may or may not be a visual sign of injury such as redness or swelling. Most often, these are injuries you cannot palpate from the outside or even see on basic medical tests such as x-rays (except a bit of arthritis). There's no blood spurting to yell, "An injury occurred here!"

However, repetitive strain injuries often look like acute injuries if the person's repetitive strain injury suddenly shows itself. An example of this is when someone who has a long-standing herniated disc (a bulging of spinal disc tissue out of its correct location) picks something up off the floor, that herniated disc now presses into a nerve, and the person falls down with sudden back pain. The issues that led up to the herniation pressing into a nerve were repetitive strain issues. The injury, however, is classified as an acute injury.

The true repetitive strain injuries, or more chronic issues, do not have an acute episode. These are the aches and pains that fluctuate in intensity, but often are associated first with specific actions (it hurts when I do this). The discomfort then moves into a period of time when it continues constantly, but gets worse with specific actions. Anywhere along this continuum, the person could be diagnosed with an RSI. The longer the discomfort has been noted, the harder it is to treat.

Continuous pain is actually the last step in a very long chain of events. Muscles start to alert the body to strain with feelings described as tired, stiff, or tight. That is a sure sign that the muscle fibers and joints have not been getting sufficient fresh blood supply or have been pushed beyond their limits. The best time for ergonomics programming to intervene so as to have the greatest likelihood of rapid success is before the pain becomes continuous. Interestingly, many companies will call this intervention "preventative." I disagree. True prevention programs ensure that the body is not stressed beyond its capability in the first place.

The Body as a Bank Account

A simplified way of looking at this concept is to imagine that each part the body has a bank account with limited funds, and each of your workers have a different amount to work with. Each of the risk factors we will look at later adds to the cost of completing a task.

Worker A's bank account looks like this: Hips have $100, back has $100, and knees have $100.

Worker B's bank account looks like this: Hips have $100, back has $50, and knees have $40.

Worker A and Worker B have had different life experiences, are in different physical conditions, and take different care of their bodies—hence, different account balances. Let's just say for the sake of this example, Worker A is a person who fits the "normal" measures. When we test Worker A's strength and endurance, Worker A falls right in the middle. Worker B falls slightly on the lower end when tested; however, Worker B can still do the job—you have seen it!

The concept of ergonomics as we are going to approach it can be simply defined as ensuring that the work requested of the employee never exceeds their bank accounts, and even better, offers the job at a discount so that the bank account doesn't run dry over the course of the day, week, or career.

For example, the job task is stacking heavy boxes. Through analysis (some of which we will get into later) we have figured out that this job is fairly hard and puts a lot strain on the knees and back. Now, I can't say how much it will cost a person—that depends on multiple factors. I can, however, say for purposes of this example, that the forces on the back exceed the accepted values and, therefore, are considered unsafe. What the field of ergonomics gives me is the tool to figure out what part of the task is too much for the body. It also gives me the tools needed to figure out what kind of improvements I can expect based on changes made to the task.

We can look at it this way (bear with me as I simplify): In this case, lifting the box once, let's say, costs the body $50 for each joint. After lifting the box once, Worker A would be okay for one more lift, but Worker B would be done for the day (and may be limping). If I change the task by storing the boxes on a platform, thereby reducing one portion of the lifting task, I can change the forces on the body. In other words, by changing how the task is done I can get it at a discount. Now, instead of costing $50 per joint, the task costs $20 per joint. Both Worker A and Worker B will last a lot longer on the job. Who doesn't love a discount!

What are the Risk Factors When Working?

The human body is a limited resource. The body can handle only so much before breaking down, making a mistake, or causing harm to other humans or machines. Ergonomics is working within the body's tolerances so that errors -- injury, failures, accidents, and breakdowns, do not occur.

Risk factors for the development of WRMSDs from repetitive tasks can be divided into six categories:

- The weight of the object being handled (load)

- How many times it is handled and for how long (duration)

- How the person is positioned when handling said object (posture)

- Other factors being applied to the body such as temperature (environment)

- The movement of the object while it is being handled (vibration or perturbations)

- The amount of contact or type of contact with the body (handles versus sharp edges)

For example, if a worker is required to lift a light object three times a day, this may not be a high-risk activity. But what would happen if we take that same light object, put it in an extremely cold environment, and have a person lift it three times per day? The risks of physical injury increase due to the environmental context including such factors as temperature, vibration, stress, and sociocultural influences. Taking the environmental context out of the equation, if the amount a person is required to lift increases to 100 pounds, even just three times per day, the risks also increase. If a person is required to lift the same 100 pounds three times per day while in a twisted position, the risks increase even more.

Conversely, consider a cashier who counts thousands of bills an hour. The loads are very light—it does not take much pinch force to move bills; however, the number of times the task is completed is very high. The risk for hand injury increases, therefore, as the repetition increases. Now, consider if that same cashier is hunched over a desk for eight hours per day while counting bills in a low-light environment. The cashier's poor posture increases the risk of hand injury because the supporting structures—i.e. the back and shoulders—are at a disadvantage due to the poor posture even though the external loads remain low.

Chapter 2: Rules of Ergonomics – Beyond "Lift with Your Knees"

"Lift with your knees and not with your back." This is a mantra repeated over and over again in training sessions and worksites around the world. However, there is much about this "rule" that isn't quite true and doesn't work. The reason to keep your back straight, or more specifically—keep your back in good postural alignment, and bend at the hips and knees to lower yourself into a squat before you pick up an object is to distribute the load properly on the spine. [3] If the object does not fit between your legs, this lift technique may in fact increase pressures on the spine. [4] [5] Also, due to poor workplace design or object design, we rarely find this technique actually used out in the field. [6]

We do a lot of consulting with employees who work in constantly varying environments that are out of their control, such as outdoors or in peoples' homes—think of any service person. There are many times when you just can't get into that squat position. Does that mean you are doomed? No, there are other aspects of the lift that you can use to mitigate risk. Can we limit duration or repetition? Change the load's position in space to limit twisting or bring the object closer to the person? This brings us to the basic rules of ergonomics.

Basic Rules of Ergonomics

This section is going to give you a few "rules" for work tasks derived from what we know about human capabilities. I'm going to skip over the calculations and measurements and just give you the equations' solutions. In the sections on office work and industrial work, I will mention some of the most commonly used tools and what they provide; however, I recommend consulting with a specialist to work out your specific measurements and solutions.

So how much is too much for the human body? I wish I could say that this question has a simple answer, but it doesn't. Remember, it is not just about the strength of an individual but the body's tolerance at its weakest points; that is, which body part has the smallest bank account. When it comes to discrete pieces of the puzzle, we do have some basic guidelines.

Load: How much is too much?

The general rule is that anything over 51 pounds (23 kg) is too much to lift. How did we come up with that number? After some long, intense studies into cadavers and other such things that many of us don't want to play with, researchers came to the basic agreement that 51 pounds creates a load pressure on the spine (think "squish factor") that can cause injury to the spinal structures. However, this load limit is greatly dependent on where the load is relative to the body, what type of grip is on the object, and other confounding variables.

Duration/repetition: How many is too much?

Sorry, there is no easy answer here. This factor is too intermingled with the other factors. We have some standards that are based on strength and heart rate; however, these would be very difficult for you to use without full resource manuals. If an environment is hot or cold, wet or dry, dark or light, the duration tolerance changes. If the task includes monotony, vibration, or shaking, such as while driving, the task tolerances can be reduced. The duration measurement has to be taken in context to be useful. Basic rule: limit duration whenever possible or break up long durations with alternate activities.

Position in space: Should you be reaching for that?

When thinking about simple ergonomics, closer to the body is best. We know that reaching for objects increases the load on the spine. We also know that reaching increases the compensatory movements of the shoulders, spine, and hips. Twisting the spine or reaching away from the body's midline, such as reaching behind the passenger seat to get something from the back seat of the car while driving, is also a movement that increases risk.

The closer the person is to "neutral" the better. To simplify, the neutral posture is where the spine is kept in the correct anatomical curves, the head is over the spine, the arms are down by the ribs, the hips are under the spine, and the legs are providing a good base of support with the knees lined up with the hips. As we move through space completing various tasks, we have to move out of neutral. Therefore, when we evaluate how to make tasks safer, we often look at how we can put the person closer to the anatomical neutral. Can we facilitate bringing the head over the shoulders, such as by raising the monitor? Can we reduce the forces on a joint, such as by changing the grip on a tool?

Posture is a very important factor that is often taken out of context during task analyses and assessment of other risk factors. Something important to remember about posture: it is influenced by a person's actions *and* the environment. How a person works should never be measured solely using simulation in a constructed environment. A person can choose to move in a certain way, such as bending at the knees or at the back. Alternatively, the environment may dictate how the person can be positioned, such as when a repair person has to reach around a prickly bush to get to an outside meter. It is easier to change the environment than it is the person's actions. Remove the bush and the person now has more options for posture. However, you may change the environment and the person will still use poor postures.

Stability and Mobility: Are you set up to succeed?

A significant factor related to posture is how the body supports movement. Each body structure, such as the arm, requires a supporting structure to function, such as the shoulder and neck. Without stability, there can be no mobility.

Case example:

Jodi works at a computer in an office cubicle most of the day. She has complained about having a constant pain in her arm. It is simple to blame the arm pain on the mouse or keyboard. After all, she complains of pain while using the mouse and keyboard, and those are low load but highly repetitive tasks she does with her arm. Research has been unable to determine which mouse or keyboard works best to prevent arm pain, or even if there is a direct link between many of the work-related musculoskeletal disorders of the upper extremity and the keyboard and mouse. This is because the research fails to take into account the other factors that influence injury, such as spinal postures or the position of the shoulder, both structures which provide stability needed to support the arm's mobility.

Think about stability and mobility this way: consider for a moment where you would put a ladder if you had to reach something on a very high shelf. Would you put in on an uneven surface or on an even surface? (See fig A and B)

Figure A: Reaching with a Stable Base

Figure B: Reaching without a Stable Base of Support

The smart person would put the ladder on a solid base of support. What injuries would you see if someone put the ladder on an uneven base of support? Well, if he fell, the list would be very long, ranging from head injury to leg fractures. What if he didn't fall but instead strained his back as a result of the lift? At no point would the injury be classified as an "uneven base of support injury to the back," although that would be a lot more accurate than classifying it as lifting injury.

The spinal and core musculature are the most basic stabilizing mechanisms we have in our body, but, unless the programs are directly related to lifting, we often ignore them when creating injury prevention programs. Base of support, or having stability, is important regardless of the position being used or the task being completed. An easy way to understand this concept is to consider the spine as the core support in a large crane. So long as that crane is upright and straight it can handle a large load (see fig C). However, if you ever saw a crane starting to bend in the middle you would probably run away as fast as you could (see fig D).

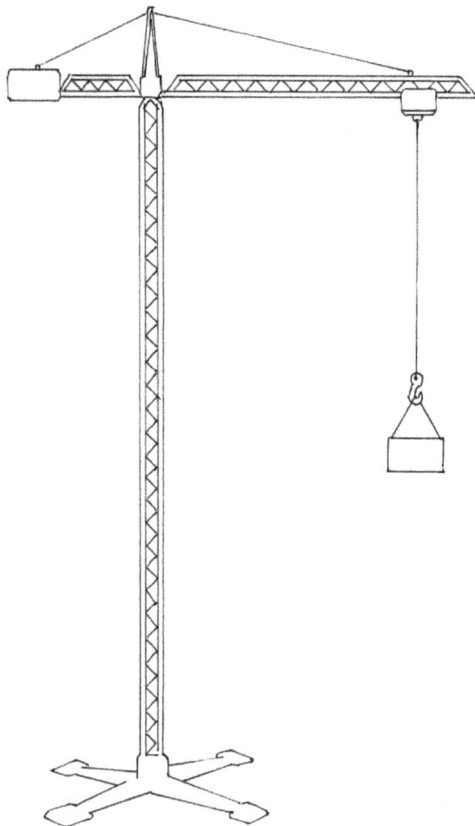

Figure C: : Stable at the Core   *Figure D: Unstable at the Core*

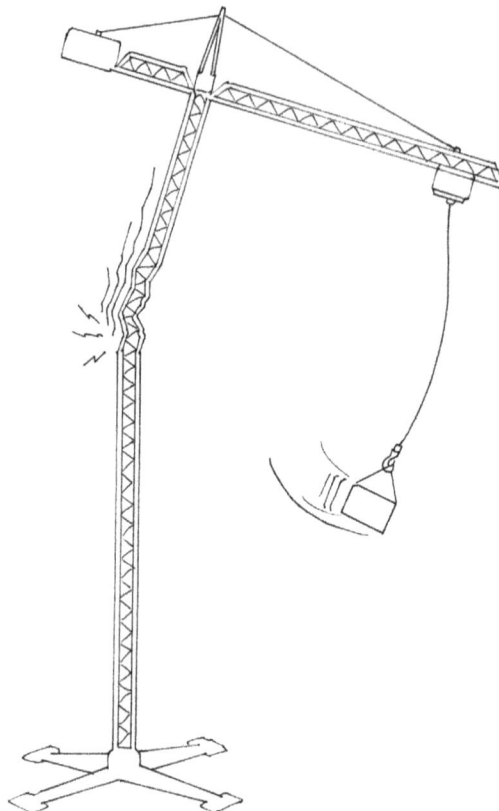

Whether through training or engineering controls, when working with people to prevent injuries, we have to help them put themselves into a posture that promotes stability whenever the task requires mobility. In standing positions, this means ensuring a solid, supportive, and even base of support, such as leveling floors or providing a non-slip, anti-fatigue mat. In sitting positions, it means providing a good seat pan (the part of the chair you sit on) and a backrest that allows for an upright supported posture.

The Reach Envelope

Base of support is only the first part of the stability to mobility relationship. The size and type of base of support also directly changes the balance of the individual. [7] [8] Stability, however, will be lost as the person moves into a position where the forces of the body are no longer directed toward the base of support, such as leaning forward to reach something. [9] Ergonomics research provides us with a concept that helps delineate how far someone can safely reach. This is called the reach envelope (see fig E).

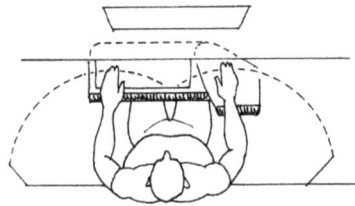

Figure E: The reach envelope

With repetitive tasks or tasks requiring force, the tools or objects related to the task should be within the person's primary reach envelope. The primary reach envelope is the arc created when the person puts their elbows up against their ribs and then internally and externally rotates their shoulders (swinging hands towards and away from lap). [10]

As the frequency of the task decreases, the range of the envelope can increase. Objects the person uses *occasionally* can be placed in the secondary zone, which is the arc created when the person reaches forward without bending the spine and then spreads their arms out to the sides. The objects that a person *rarely* uses can be placed in the zone where he or she must climb on something while completing the reach. When I teach this to employees, I use the concept of *'power zones'* (see fig F).

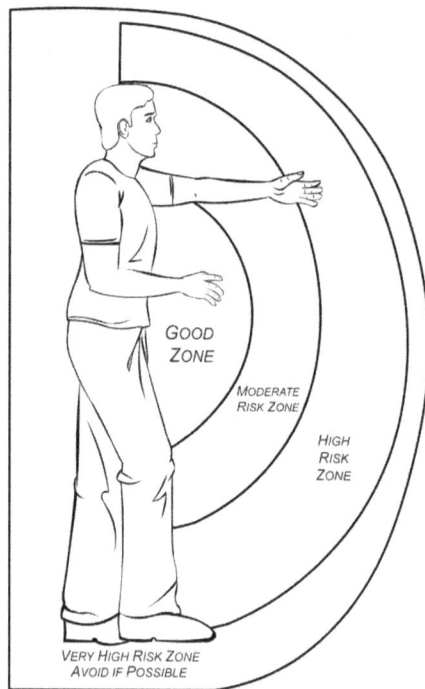

Figure F: Power Zones

How to Find the Risk Factors

Root cause analysis is the process of looking for the chain of events that led up to an injury or incident. In addition to the action that caused the injury, root cause analysis often gives us a good idea of the context surrounding a problem and an awareness of seemingly innocuous events that actually may have led up to the problem. It is important to note that traditional root cause analyses occur after an injury or incident. However, with ergonomics, we often also run the same process on areas identified as having a *potential* for injury or incident, that is, prevention. We want to know how we might get or have gotten into a situation that exceeds the human body's tolerance. This is extremely important when we discuss the process of solving the problems identified.

Why, Why, Why

I believe one of first questions we learn as children is actually the best question. Parents around the globe can attest to the patience needed for that ever present *why?* Children have no problem asking why anything and asking as many times as they can regardless of how logical the first answer. Why nap now? Because you are tired. But why? Because I said so. But why?

When we become adults, we often feel we have the answer, so *why* no longer becomes the pressing question. We switch to *when* (so we can get places on time), *how* (so we do not make mistakes), *where* (to find what we need), and so on. However, asking the question *why something happens* is one of the most sure-fire ways to dig in and find how best to understand a problem, so that a solution can be discovered. *Why* is the question I ask myself over and over while striving to find solutions for my clients. It is the question I am going to challenge you with in this book. And I warn you, the answer may not come as easily as you would like.

For example, a question often asked after an injury is: Why did that injury occur? What was the root cause of the injury? Unfortunately, I have seen time and again when the *why* is answered with the easy way out. Let us take an injury that happens with alarming frequency in any field where people have to get in and out of a vehicle on a regular basis—a twisted ankle. Why did that person twist an ankle? Easy answer: They were not looking where they were putting their foot— inattention.

> I hereby challenge you to find the not easy answer.

After seeing a number of these twisted ankle injuries, I found it hard to accept that all of these injuries were caused by people simply not looking where they were going. If so, the solution would be as simple as telling people to look before they get out of the cab. Would that really work?

So let's do a little experiment: The WHY?

Injury: Twisted ankle after getting out of vehicle.

Easy answer: Inattention. Now, keep going...

Why #1: Why are people not paying attention?

Possible answer: They are looking up at where they are going instead of down where their feet go.

Why #2: Why are people not looking where they are going when we have told them that twisted ankles are happening regularly?

Possible answer: Because we pay them to do whatever it is they are headed towards, not to look at their feet, and we want them focused on what their job is – the reason they are there.

Why #3: Why does focus on the future job task take precedence over not hurting themselves?

Other possible answer: Because it was dark outside and they were trying to be sure no one was sneaking up on them.

Why #4: Why were they in a situation where the area is dark?

Starting to get the picture? The goal is to ask WHY at least 7 times to be sure you have actually reached the correct conclusion. Yes, sometimes you can sound like a tired two year old, but I wholeheartedly recommend this concept. (One would hope that you find tactful ways of asking the why.)

Why is it important in the case example of twisted ankles to ask why so many times? The easy answer, inattention, would lead us to hold a quick meeting and tell everyone to look where they are going, watch where they are stepping, and *pay attention.* Hate to tell you, but I speak from experience, that this will not reduce your injuries. Why? Well…we will get to that in the rest of the book.

The next obvious question: Why are we talking about *why* and not ergonomics programming, like the title says?

Ergonomics as a concept is fairly simple, and most of you will use experts for the details. The problem is that programming around ergonomics, safety, health, and other of those "good for you" topics often fail. How many smoking cessation programs have bit the dust after a lot of cash has been invested? In fact, they fail so often that many question the purpose of putting on programming in the first place, except that it checks the box and makes the government happy. However, they do not have to fail. Let me say that again—these are programs that do not have to fail if done correctly, rechecked often, and modified as different *whys* are discovered. I would really like your program to succeed. Why? Success equals employees who can continue to work, continue to produce, and perhaps even more importantly, work for you for as long as they want—not as long as they can.

For example, take the case where we have people being injured while carrying a heavy box. The ergonomics assessment has been completed, and measurements show that the weight of the box does not exceed our levels of tolerance.

So why is there an injury?

It turns out that the box is being carried down a set of stairs. As we move on uneven surfaces, our bodies have to work harder (e.g. carrying a box down stairs costs more than carrying it on a level surface), and we see awkward movement patterns start to appear. Therefore, it most likely that reducing the weight of the box would not solve the problem. We may have to chase this injury back in its history of development:

- Why was the box at the top of the stairs to begin with?

- Are the box contents something that actually needs to be brought down stairs?

- And so on.

The Occupational Safety and Health Administration (OSHA) is a government agency that enforces safe working conditions. It provides guidelines to keep workplaces free of slips, trips, falls, burns, etc., and dictates how these injuries should be recorded. Injuries, their classification, extent, severity, and cause are recorded in an OSHA 300 Log. [11] The log is important because it influences how injuries are documented. However, the log also is a limiting factor since it does not require an in-depth analysis of root cause. It only requires that a cause be listed. Also, strains and sprains--the injuries we are most interested in for the purposes of this book -- are not documented unless "they result from a slip, trip, fall, or other similar accidents." [12] In other words, there must be a discrete event that occurs in order for it to be recordable, in contrast to a repetitive strain complaint with no discernible acute injury.

What makes these injuries even harder to solve with "generic" solutions is that the cause of the injury may not actually have anything to do with the part of the body that was injured. Think back to Jodi with her arm pain. A common repetitive strain disorder that presents as pain in the arm is called lateral epicondylitis, a.k.a. tennis elbow. This injury is often associated with using the mouse for long periods.

The root cause analysis often ends here:

> Cause = using the mouse.

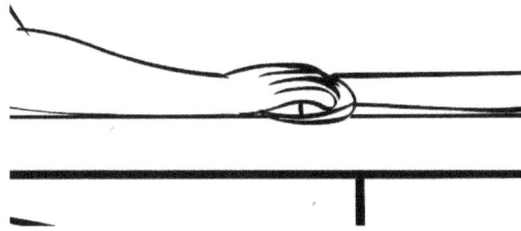

Figure G: The mouse hand

However, it is rarely that simple, which is why changing the mouse does not solve the problem. Each body structure, such as the arm, requires a supporting structure to function, such as the shoulder and neck. As discussed earlier, without stability there can be no mobility. This is a basic tenet of movement that plays a vital role in understanding work-related musculoskeletal disorders. [13] However, it is often neglected when the observed injury does not relate to the body's core stabilizers, such as the back and legs. Therefore, lateral epicondylitis cannot solely be attributed to mouse use. Instead, very often the person's forward head posture with rounded shoulders plays a role in that injury.

Figure H: The whole picture

A flashy new mouse will not solve the problem. What must be addressed is the leaning and reaching. We often refer to this forward posture as a *turtle posture*.

> Look around your office. (No really, you probably need a break right about now, so you should take this opportunity to do a quick walk around your offices. Just don't forget to come back.) Do you see people sitting at their desks leaning forward looking like turtles or reaching out in front of themselves or to the sides like a chicken's wings? Knowing what you now know – do your employees look comfortable and supported?

Can you find the turtles in your office?

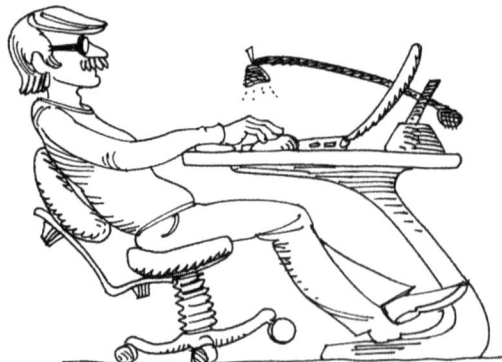

Chapter 3: Is the Expense Worth It?

Safety programs, and therefore ergonomics programs, *do* cost money. I often warn people that they can expect a good ergonomics program will cost the most in the first few years of program development and launch. However, you need to think of all of these programs as investments in your human resource. [14] In the long view, an investment in ergonomics increases worker productivity and allows your employees to work better, longer, while cutting costs to your bottom line that you probably aren't even aware of. [*] A good ergonomics program will address problems that you probably don't know you have and that may be impacting your bottom line far more than you realize, even if you already have an injury prevention program in place.

Current estimates put return on investment for good ergonomics programs at around 1:6. For every dollar invested, the industry standard is around six dollars saved. This combines money saved on not having your insurance premiums go up, decreased absences, and improved productivity.

How do you find your hidden costs?

The costs that are most often used to calculate injury prevention program necessity, success, or failure are:

- Occupational Safety and Health Administration logs on workplace injuries

- Worker's compensation insurance base costs

- Worker's compensation claims. [15] [†]

---

* - *OSHA has recently published a very well written white paper on how occupational safety and health should be put into the same category as sustainability investments. You can read the full report here: https:// www.osha.gov/sustainability/docs/OSHA_sustainability_paper.pdf*

† - *This is mainly true in the United States. If you have questions about this anywhere else in the world, please send me an email at naomi@workinjuryfree.com.*

But these data do not tell the whole story of employee injuries, nor do they tell you the real costs to your company. The problems we are addressing take a little more digging.

The injuries most often reported as workers' compensation claims usually have a specific associated event—someone stuck their hand in a machine, someone fell down, someone collapsed. You may not have high injury rates or workers' compensation costs, but don't let that fool you. The RSI we are discussing are hidden in your health insurance, sick leave, absenteeism, presenteeism, "special" equipment costs, and general worker productivity and happiness. Consider these statistics:

- The National Institutes on Occupational Safety and Health (NIOSH), the United States federal government agency responsible for research and recommendations related to workplace safety, reports that an estimated 3.4 million emergency room visits in one year were related to workplace injuries or illnesses. [16] Of those injuries, approximately 53 percent were categorized as sprains and strains, with a few puncture injuries thrown in. Most of the sprains and strains affected the trunk, which includes, in their definition, the shoulder as well as the back, chest. and abdomen, and lower extremities.

- The World Health Organization (WHO) estimates that, within all industrialized countries, one-third of all health-reason absences from work are due to work-related musculoskeletal disorders. [17]

- The Bureau of Labor Statistics (BLS), which collects information related to labor issues in the U.S., reported that the median amount of time a worker was out of work due to an injury is eight days.[18] In that same report, BLS announced that the rate of WRMSDs was increasing.

Something to realize about these metrics is that they only include injuries <u>that have been reported as a workplace injury</u>. Not included are the "injuries" that your employees took directly to their healthcare providers. My company helped several international firms complete a recent survey. [‡] In it we found that an average of 60-80% of the population surveyed [§] had one or more musculoskeletal disorders that affected their productivity that they had <u>not</u> reported to their supervisors. Your employees are not taking these WRMSD's into the workers' compensation world and they are not informing you of their problems. Therefore, you are shelling out money for treatment, but you never get the opportunity to make a constructive change to address these costs, which is a lose-lose situation for both the company and the employee.

To make matters within the workplace even more dire, the "work related" injuries are not always directly work related. The workers themselves bring with them from their lives outside of work many factors that affect injury rates and the ability to avoid injuries.

Consider the risks associated with household tasks such as mowing the lawn, clearing downed trees, or shoveling snow. Whether we are aware of it, employees may be arriving at work already injured from a weekend of yard work or helping a friend move. What about the physical and psychosocial toll that caring for others places on a caregiver? The number of people caring for older parents, sick parents, or siblings and children with disabilities is rapidly growing in the US. We know that health care workers have some of the highest rate of <u>reported</u> injuries; studies have also shown that they have a very high rate of <u>not reporting</u> injuries. What can we extrapolate, based on these numbers, regarding the risks involved

---

‡ - *Sorry, this was a confidential study. We can't give you specifics of who was involved, just the blinded results.*

§ - *We had around 11,000 responses, which constituted over 20% response rate from each company—from a statistical standpoint, we were happy with this response rate and felt comfortable giving each company generalized conclusions.*

with tasks such as caring for children or elderly parents by the average untrained caregiver?

Other problems your employees bring with them to work include obesity, diabetes, and heart disease, all of which are running rampant in the U.S. population.[19] (From our international surveys mentioned earlier, we are also seeing those problems in many other regions that do not have such detailed health care data, so if you are reading this book in another country—sorry, you cannot dismiss this.) Why should you care? If a person who works for you is obese and has diabetes that has caused peripheral neuropathy in his legs (numbness or tingling feeling in the feet), he has an increased risk of foot injury on the job. If he also has undiagnosed sleep apnea, a condition where he stops breathing for brief periods at night due to a collapsing of the trachea, he is not getting enough rest at night to sustain optimal daily function.[20] This will decrease his situational awareness and, therefore, decrease his ability to avoid injury—an injury you pay for in the end.

> Consider this: When was the last time you took a good look at how much you are spending on back pain, neck pain, carpal tunnel syndrome, hand pain, shoulder pain, and eye strain through your primary health insurance? How about lost time when your employees are at their chiropractors, general doctors, physical and occupational therapists, massage therapists, and acupuncturists instead of being at work? I can tell you, the dollar figure is a lot larger than you would like it to be.

So, how can you get a handle on what these costs really are and how much you can expect an ergonomics program to save your company in the long run? A direct way of getting some of this information is to just ask. Surveys are not perfect because the data are subjective, but they can still give you some idea. A well-designed health risk analysis/assessment is a very useful tool for probing how healthy your employees think they are.

Steps I recommend taking before, during, and after implementing an ergonomics program to get objective data include:

- Determine how much your workers' compensation insurance cost has changed over the last few years.

- Find out whether your workers' compensation insurance provides stipends or bonuses for having injury prevention programs--any and all, not just ergonomics.

- Evaluate your primary health insurance data for the number of people with WRMSD diagnoses. No, you are not saying that these diagnoses were caused by work; you are simply finding out if you have a workforce population who is working at the end of their resources. Do *not* get data that has identifiers! You do not want to get sued.

- Evaluate your time-off data if you have it. This is a little easier with shift workers. Many workplaces with salaried employees that do not work specific shifts allow workers to leave for a few hours so long as the time is made up sometime. The information on time off is really lost to the employer—something to think about.

Once you have done a pre-assessment of where your costs are, what should you expect from your programs? Later in the book, we will discuss what makes up a good program. However, I want to take a moment to talk about realistic expectations. I would love to say that ergonomics can solve all problems. If you have employees who already have a great many injuries, they will continue to have discomfort regardless of what we do, although we have consistently shown that ergonomics programs can reduce the overall level of discomfort. However, what we are looking for is to reduce the overall risk and therefore reduce the likelihood of these discomforts becoming part of your bottom line.

Part 2: How to Design Ergonomics Programs

Chapter 4: Program Components

Let's review the general components of an ergonomics program.

- Evaluation and measurement

- Reporting

- Address concerns through:

  1. Engineering controls

  2. Administrative controls

  3. Behavioral controls, including training

- Reinforcement

Evaluation and Measurement

Measuring the scope of the problem, the forces at work, the stressors, the key stakeholders' requests, and an analysis of movements or behaviors, all fall under this category. The evaluation tools can range from surveys to in-depth 3D imaging, depending on the company's needs. In the office and industrial sections, we will review the specific evaluations typically used for the respective situations, and in the Appendices, I give you details of some of the more common assessment tools. Many programs that fail do not include an evaluation component, only a correcting or training component. The choice to skip the evaluation phase usually has more to do with budget than need.

It is important to note, however, that evaluations and measurements must be correct for the task being completed and interpreted correctly within the limitations of the tools. The results can be interpreted or generalized differently depending on who is doing the evaluation or how the measurement tool was designed. Each tool has its limitations. For example, most of the office evaluation tools see the body in sections: the upper body, the neck, the trunk, etc. The tool itself cannot measure the effect of changing the position of the trunk as it relates to the position of the upper body. Conversely, one of the common lifting equations can measure the effectiveness of different task modifications because you can plug in different factors. However, that equation cannot tell you what would happen if the person uses a tool. That equation only sees the body's movements and does not take into account what is in the person's hands.

Reporting

Every program must have some component of feedback for the stakeholders. This can be as simple as a list of attendance at safety meetings or as complex as a lengthy presentation with graphs and renderings. Your reporting needs will depend on how you wrote your program goals and the components you have in your program. Our programs often include a visual presentation of significant findings of evaluations to key stakeholders as part of the reporting process. Some companies prefer reports to include a synopsis page, or "what is the bottom line," so they have a summary that can be distributed without the clutter associated with the detailed findings. You will have to decide what works best for your stakeholders.

Reports are often provided after evaluations, program implementation, specific events or trainings, and after program milestones. There is no standardized format for any of these reports within the profession.

How Does Ergonomics Address the Problems?

There are a variety of methods for actually correcting a problem or, if you can't completely correct it, at least somewhat reducing the risks. There are three broad categories of methods used in ergonomics to mitigate risks: engineering controls, administrative controls, and behavioral or individual controls. Each method has a purpose and should be considered for every risk identified—do not separate these methods out and consider them an either/or solution. Engineering controls are the most effective and where you should begin to mitigate every risk.

Engineering controls

The first type of ergonomic intervention is to change the tool or task itself. This type of intervention deals with the problem by making a physical change, or engineering out the problem. That physical change either brings the task or tools into the safe parameters for a human worker or places it so far out of the abilities of the human that a mechanical assist is justified. There is an old adage in ergonomics: if you can't make it lighter, make it too heavy. What do we mean? Let's say we have a situation where someone needs to lift a 50-pound bag constantly. We do the mathematics; we do the measurements; and we find that lifting the 50-pound bag regularly is too much for the human body. We then have two options:

1. Make the bag lighter: Perhaps if the person were only lifting 10 pounds regularly, it wouldn't be as much of a problem.

2. We could also do the exact reverse and make the bag 1,000 pounds. This would greatly exceed our lifting limits. It would also make it more reasonable to bring in a machine that would lift that bag, instead of having the human do it.

Worker advocacy groups are often concerned that ergonomics will replace all human workers with machines—after all, machines have much higher tolerances. Having worked in the field for over 10 years, I can tell you I have never replaced a human being with a machine. No human beings have lost their jobs because of any analysis I've done. Instead, what happens is that the human beings are used more efficiently. The human beings are used instead for their brains, their knowledge, and their experience, things you could never teach a machine.

Engineering the stapler

Look at the stapler on your desk. Does it have a flat bottom and rounded top, lying flat lengthwise along the table? How do you think it is meant to be used? Is it supposed to be pressed down into the table or picked up and squeezed?

Staplers were designed to be pressed down into the table using body leverage instead of hand strength—smart design to limit hand fatigue. But what happened?

People have a tendency to pick a stapler up and squeeze it instead of standing up to press it down into the desk.

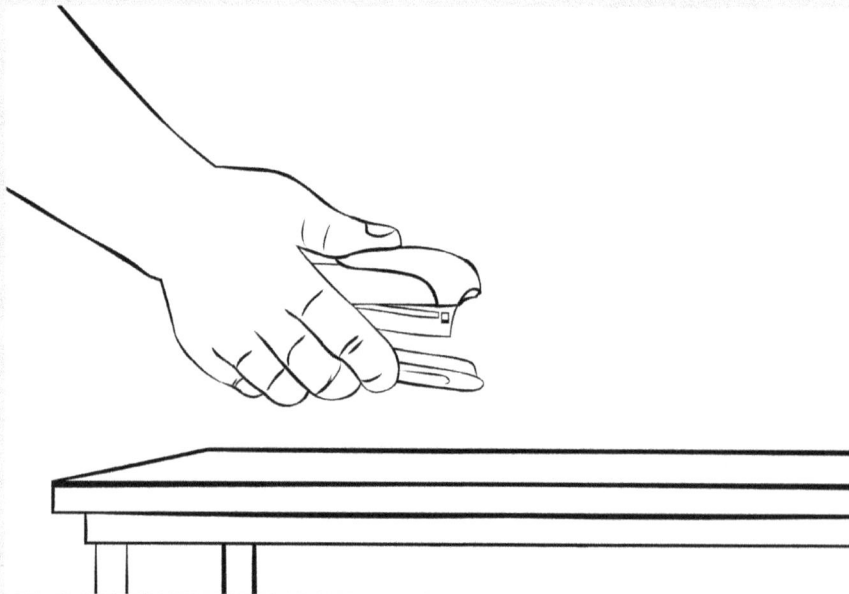

Figure I: Using a stapler incorrectly

People who use a stapler a lot often complain of hand pain.

Problem 1: The bottom of the stapler has a flat sharp edge so that it is stable on the table.
Problem 2: It takes a lot of force to squeeze a staple through a big stack of papers.

A company came along and said, "We can build a better stapler," and made a stapler that stands on its end and has soft rounded edges on all sides.

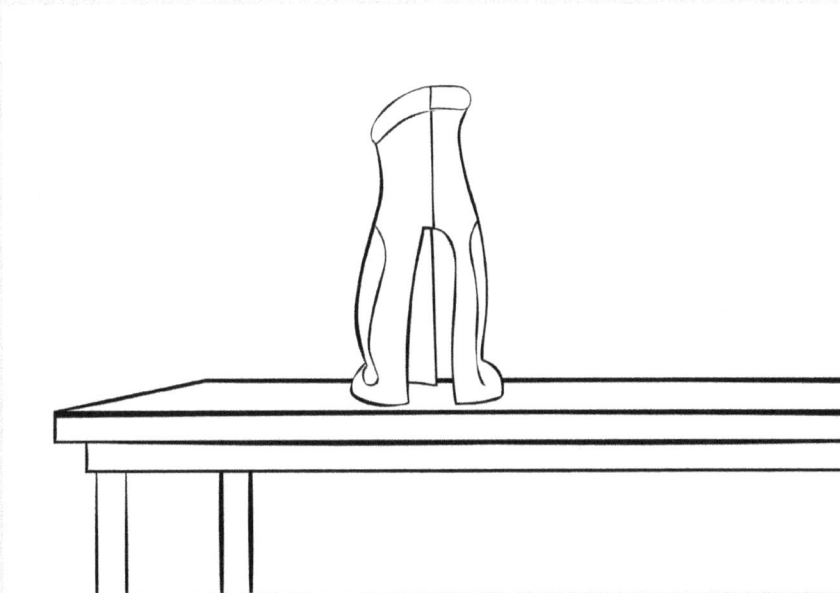

Figure J: A stapler to squeeze

Problem solved? Nope.

People are complaining of hand pain because of the same problem they had in the first place—squeezing! If people had been told why the stapler was designed the way it was, with a flat bottom, and people were using it correctly as it was designed, there would be no hand pain.

Of course, you could just go out and get an electric stapler.

Administrative control

Administrative controls are modifications to the rules and regulations or the work behaviors expected by management for the employees. For example, we may institute a job rotation schedule when the job has been identified as having risk that cannot be modified by an engineering solution. Therefore, we reduce the amount of time that each employee may be experiencing that risk.

Administrative controls work well only when there is not an interfering sociocultural influence. For example, when you have a job rotation schedule affecting individuals who identify themselves as strong and powerful, and they perceive that their work behaviors are being judged for their stamina, employees are not willing to comply with job rotations.

Case example:

I was out on a job site recently where the potential for musculoskeletal strain was so high that everyone there stopped the job in the middle to think about alternative approaches that might make this job safer. After considering multiple options, we decided there was no way of making the job safer. However, the job had to get done because the public was at risk. Everyone there agreed that no one should be doing the job for too long, so as to reduce individual exposure.

The supervisor got down in the hole we were working in and started working on that job. After about 30 minutes of hard labor, his crew members told him it was time to come out of the hole. He had been working too long, and he needed a break. His response was, "Just a little bit more. I've almost got it." He repeated this excuse until he got so tired that he had no choice but to get out of the hole.

His next crewmember got in and proceeded to work for too long. The supervisor was saying it was time to get out of the hole, and the crewmember responded with, "Just a little longer. I've almost got it."

So what was actually happening in this situation? The sociocultural pressure to not give up on a job, the internal pressure to not let a job get the better of them, and the frustration at not being able to get the job done, all combined to influence the workers to completely reject the agreed-upon administrative controls. This is the difficult part about administrative controls. They look very good on paper and they work well in theory. When administrative controls are tried in the field, however, they can be very hard to implement.

Administrative controls, however, work very well in a controlled environment such as a call center or a manufacturing line. There, it becomes routine to know that at a set point in time or after a set period of time, something about the work changes. That time cue stays the same and a compliance habit is developed.

Behavioral controls and individual controls

We often rely on the individual employee to make decisions to improve his behavior or work tolerances, such as through physical training or self-help classes. The idea is that if I can't engineer out the problem, and I can't administer out the problem, I'm going to rely on the individual. The behavioral control and individual control category is very broad, and many purists in the ergonomics world actually reject this category as even being part of ergonomics. They postulate that engineering controls are the only tools that should be used. However, when training programs are included in ergonomics programs, we consider this a behavioral control. Another example of behavioral controls or individual controls are programs that teach resiliency under stress, such as effective time management or creating a cooperative and respectful workplace, in an effort to reduce the cognitive burden of a job. Programs that teach resiliency to stressors in an effort to reduce the cognitive load of a job are another example of behavioral controls or individual controls.

Programs that include physical training or eyesight testing for glasses would fit under the individual controls category. Fire departments and police departments cannot change anything about the job itself since it deals with other human beings and equipment that must be heavy to do the job safely. Instead, fire and police departments have physical fitness requirements to ensure that their employees have the physical strength needed to complete the essential functions of the jobs. Behavioral and individual controls often are considered a last resort for ergonomics programs because they rely on human beings taking specific actions or improving personal attributes.

In my opinion, however, the behavioral component *needs* to exist regardless of any other changes that are made. I believe that the behavioral component is the most important feature of a successful ergonomics program. The behavioral component is how you achieve buy-in from your employees. This component is also necessary to ensure that your employees correctly implement any engineering or administrative control. It is, admittedly, the hardest component to achieve. I have personally observed people take engineering controls, that should have worked to reduce risk, and use them in a way that increases the risk beyond even the original risk level. There is often a gap between how the engineers plan a modification and how the employees later work with that modification. When behavioral changes are accounted for in an ergonomics program they can help close that gap. Think of the behavioral control as a time to train employees on modifications or controls. Keep that in mind as we continue.

One of the biggest "ah ha" moments of my career was during a safety training class in which we were going over the protective equipment that must be worn, according to OSHA standards, when using a chainsaw. This training was done at the workplace with people who use chainsaws frequently at work It was done by a chainsaw safety expert who used to work in the field with a chainsaw, just like the people listening to the workshop, so no chance of "I know my job better than you do" bias. In fact, the workshop included a demonstration of what happens if the chainsaw slips and hits a leg--played by a tree branch in this demonstration, versus hitting the protective pants, worn by the tree branch, as well. After all of that, one of the participants asked--and this is a direct quote: "But what [protective equipment] do I have to use when using a chainsaw at home? Because I don't like wearing the pants." My jaw dropped. I did not know that cutting off your leg at work was a different injury than cutting off your leg at home. I figured it must be since the person was willing to take a greater risk of cutting off his leg at home than at work. Stepping back, what does that tell us about the safety program and safety culture at this work place?

Chapter 5: Pre-Planning for Your Program

Getting Input from Employees

One of the biggest mistakes that companies make when developing new programs is they work from the top down without inviting the participation of the employees who will be affected. An engineering change will be done to *their* workspace. *They* will need to change how *they* are working. The line employees are given very little power to control change and, thus, the employees have little to no reason to embrace any changes. However, if used properly, planning an ergonomics program is an excellent way to give employees a method of promoting change in their own workplace. In the psychological world, we call this having a *locus of control*, a feeling of having control over an environment.

Having worked with hundreds of employees, I can tell you that one of the biggest complaints I hear out in the field, on the line, or in the office, is that management does not respect the knowledge an employee has about his own job. Employees are often the last people asked for input when the company wants to make changes. This approach does not result in effective change. The effect instead is to teach employees to keep their mouths shut. In the world of programming for ergonomics, we call a program that excels at bringing the line employees into the loop "participatory ergonomics," interactive programs, or employee-driven programs. Programs that focus on creating an engineering change—in other words, programs that put a new tool or piece of equipment in place in order to reduce injuries—are very effective. However, that effectiveness is completely negated if the employees do not accept the change.

Another thought experiment:

Your company says to you: We are going to completely upgrade the computers and change all of the programs. You then come in on Monday and find that your computer has been completely changed.

All your files are there somewhere, but you don't know how to get to them. All of your programs are there, but they are now reversed. How would that make you feel as employee, especially if you were highly productive with your old piece of software?

This scenario has happened a lot over the last couple of years as programs and computers continue to evolve. Now, if you were raised with constantly changing computer programs, where every month there was a new app out there that you willingly downloaded, it's not that big a deal. However, for the majority of the population, suddenly changing a program they have used for a long time without asking for an opinion—that is a severe blow. How do we mitigate that? How about asking YOU, the person who uses the program, whether or not the program you're currently using works? How about asking if you want an upgrade?

Let's change the scenario, just a tiny bit. You have been using software XYZ for the last 10 years to organize all of your HR files. You're very comfortable with it and it works. There are a few things that you might have liked it to do better, but you have gotten used to the way it is. Your company comes to you and says: We are looking at new software. XYZ is no longer going to be supported and we'd like to find a better option. What do you recommend this better option have as its primary features? What features in the old program XYZ did you use the most? What were the biggest things that, if you had total control over the software, you would change? What if, then, the company came to you and said: Here are two potential programs. Will you please test them?

You, as the HR specialist who has been working with the program, are therefore identified as a master user. Regardless of the outcome of the situation, at this point you already feel that you are part of a team identifying a solution.

Do I Have to Do Everything at Once?

Regardless of the types of controls being used or the type of work being addressed, I like to divide ergonomics programs into three phases of implementation to address both preventative and reactive situations. The reactive components come first. These address the most pressing concerns of people with injury or near-injury. After employees with pressing issues are taken care of, the program can focus on preventative measures.

Throughout your ergonomics program, there must be standard policies developed on risk management for employees. Policies to address prompt and thorough response or reaction to an injury to prevent others from harm requires two parts. The intervention policy addresses risks identified after someone has reported an actual injury. The rapid response policy addresses issues that have not yet progressed to an injury, but have demonstrated poor effects on worker well-being. For example, someone is complaining of discomfort, but has not yet filed a workers' compensation claim or reported a disability or diagnosis. By having both of these levels of policy in place, you are stating a commitment to address issues quickly and protecting your human resource.

The prevention component focuses on your commitment and protocol for addressing areas of risk that you have identified prior to injury occurring, such as when initiating a new job, tool, or process—you are making it a policy of checking to be sure the planned change doesn't do harm. This can include a review of furniture and layout when designing a new office or a full 3D rendering of how a new tool will change the movements along a manufacturing line.

The three phases may follow sequentially or overlap based on the company's needs and abilities:

1. **Intervention**: This portion of the program addresses jobs or tasks that have a history of injuring employees.

2. Rapid response: All of our programs include a method that allows anybody in the company to report feelings of physical fatigue or aches that could potentially signal an upcoming injury. In other words, we create a method where all employees from all levels of work feel comfortable approaching someone within the company (the ergonomics team, managers, safety managers, or HR managers) to resolve problems early so that they do not develop into injuries.

3. Prevention: This is where we as the experts, and your employees as the newly trained observers, are going around the company looking for areas of potential risk. Reducing risk is equivalent to working smarter, not harder. Working smarter is a concept most people can get behind.

Each action, regardless of whether it was done as an intervention or prevention, must be followed up with a frequent, systematic, and relevant reminder program. As we will discuss in both the office and industrial sections, reminder programs can range from direct in-person visits from a manager or ergonomics professional to an electronic software pinging the employee on a regular basis with messages and actionable items. First, it is very easy for your employees to slip into old habits and postures. Habits are followed without thought; new behaviors require attention. When an employee demonstrates correct posture at a computer workstation today, he will still need reinforcement over time to integrate it into general habits for every day. Second, it is very difficult for people to generalize new postures and movement patterns into various situations. For example, if the employee demonstrates that she knows how to correctly lift a jackhammer, bucket, and pipe during the trainings, she will need reinforcement of the trainings when she goes into the field and has to lift a drill, bag, and box.

What Do You Want to Achieve?

To create a successful program, you will first need to assess what goals you want to achieve with the program. As you already know, any good program has metrics to measure its success. When it comes to an ergonomics program, there are a few very common metrics. The most common has to do with injury reduction. Now, this goal has a number of very deceptive traps that are easy to get caught in. Let's take a look at it.

The employees at Company A have many injuries. Therefore, the company's goal for their ergonomics program is to reduce injuries. They write the following goal for this year: We will have zero injuries. This goal is passed to the managers. The managers put a sign up on the wall: "Goal = Zero Injuries." It is one of the most common posters I have seen in organizations, closely followed by the poster: "It has been X number of days since the last injury." These posters really are about reducing the number of injuries *reported*, not the number of injuries that actually occur.

What we have found is that when you put up a poster that says the goal is zero injuries, employees see that in a different way than management. The manager's goal is for their group to experience zero injuries because getting hurt is a bad thing, obviously. Remember, the ergonomics program is aimed at repetitive strain injuries. Here's the trap. Repetitive strain injuries are not easy to see and are often hidden from management in primary health care costs and sick leave. These are not injuries that require calling 911. These are not injuries that have blood spewing or necessitate production lines shutting down. These are the injuries that require a level of trust between the management and employees to assure they will be reported.

Please don't misunderstand. Having zero injuries is a good goal. However, what happens when an employee sees that if they have zero injuries for that month they will get, let's be simplistic, a pizza party? If they really want that pizza party, they will do everything in their power to have zero injuries. The last thing you want to have happen with your ergonomics program is a reduction in the *reports* of injury. This further hides repetitive strain injuries from management.

So if we already know that getting employees to report musculoskeletal injuries early and consistently is difficult, do we really want to put forth a metric that further hides injuries?

> One thing that makes doing office ergonomics evaluations so pleasurable for me is when workers in neighboring cubicles start sneaking looks over the divider to see what is going on with their colleague. The neighbors start listening in and trying to figure out how to use the levers on their chairs or move their monitor. The primary question posed to me: how do I arrange to have you come to me? In my opinion, referrals make the best clients. Once the neighbors see that their colleague is expressing pleasure at being comfortable, they want in on the fun! The ergonomics program spreads organically and there is increased buy-in from staff.

Interestingly, when we take a look at good ergonomics programs, ones that have great success at reducing injuries, the most common result of program implementation is that injury reporting *increases*. Of course, this increase in reporting often causes companies great concern. Having more injuries reported is perceived as a bad thing. Notice I say "reported" and "perceived." Which is worse, to have employees experiencing injuries that affect productivity but that are hidden from you? Or to have employees with injuries that affect productivity reported to you?

I warn my clients that they will end up spending more on ergonomics programs in the beginning. As problems are solved, discomforts are addressed and risks are mitigated, the company will need less ergonomic intervention. That is primarily because ergonomics programs at the beginning phase are fact-finding. They are digging deep under the layers of your company to try and find all of these issues that you knew were there—otherwise you wouldn't have started this program.

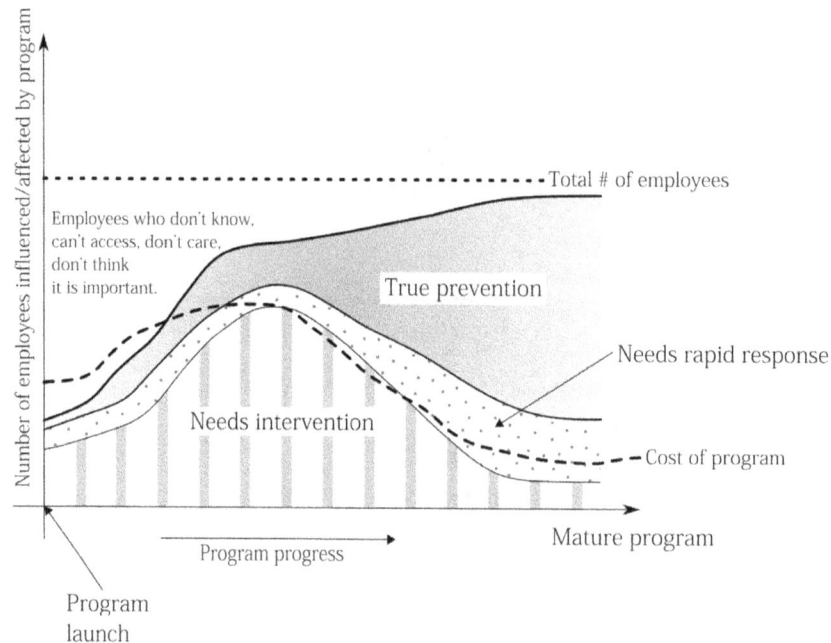

Figure K: Program process

So "zero injuries" may not be the right goal for you to put in writing. Let us say that, instead of zero injuries every month, the program would like to see a reduction in acute injuries with an increased reporting of risks or discomfort. The goal is to get more reporting by the employees, to get more reporting by the managers, and most importantly, to get people looking for areas of risk. A long-term goal may be that you would like to have zero actual injuries. But a better company goal may revolve around productivity. You can have an ergonomics goal that says we would like to improve comfort in order to improve productivity. Or in the reverse: We will improve productivity by implementing X number of changes.

The two key elements of good ergonomics program goals are:

A: The goals revolve around identifying risk and mitigating that risk. Therefore, the program will result in lowering the likelihood of injury.

B: The goals revolve around involving all of the key stakeholders in the company, not just the employees.

Be SMART about your goals:

S – Goals need to be significant to your company or they will not drive change

M – Goals should be meaningful and measureable; otherwise, you will not know if programs are worth doing

A – Goals need to be attainable. Since ergonomics and musculoskeletal problems are very complex issues, do not overreach and, therefore, fail.

R – Keep goals results-oriented so that everyone knows where this program is going.

T – Set a timeframe for when you will come back and check a goal or when you think a goal will be met.

Here are some potential ergonomic goals:

- Increase the number of risk areas identified within tasks or jobs with high workers' compensation claims within the next six months from zero to 10.

- Increase employee participation in risk-identifying activities for at least three tasks in the next six months as demonstrated by employees handing in risk forms.

- Increase participation in ergonomics program activities by managers and key stakeholders from zero to 3 of 5 activities within the next year. Participation is measured by attendance in meetings, participation in risk analyses, participation in educational seminars, response to reports, etc.

- Increase safe ergonomic practices observed and reported by managers by 50 percent over the next three years.

- Managers have in their personal goals to note and reinforce at least one positive risk-reducing behavior with each of their staff members each month/quarter/year, such as scheduling/participating in walking meetings, reviewing ergonomic principles with new staff, offering to trade when job rotation is needed, etc.

Look at each of these goals and think about how each one contains the elements of a good ergonomics program goal and are also good SMART goals.

Once again, realize that at the beginning of the program, you will most likely find people complaining more about discomfort than they did before the program started. But the goal is not to reduce complaints; it is to reduce the injuries and discomfort that are the cause of the complaints.

What Do I Do About People Who Already Hurt?

Ergonomics is a science and set of tools that are used to prevent injuries or deal with jobs and tasks that are associated with injuries. As discussed earlier, ergonomics can be used as part of an intervention when an injury has occurred on a specific job or task. Alternatively, it can be used as a preventative measure with a job or task that has the potential to cause injury. With both prevention and intervention, ergonomics is concerned with addressing the needs of the masses—reducing the risk for everyone who does the job or task.

Ergonomics also is used as a tool to better adapt a workplace or task to a specific individual's needs. This is most commonly referred to as making accommodations—bridging the gap between an individual's abilities and the job tasks. This difference in the individual's abilities and the abilities of others in the organization can be due to a pre-existing illness or injury or due to a work-related injury. Not all ergonomic experts get involved in accommodations; however, my occupational therapy background and expertise means I am frequently called in to address these concerns. Therefore, I feel it is important to address how ergonomics is used in the field of accommodations. I also will briefly mention some of the regulations that may influence your program design.

This is where I remind you that I am not an attorney and cannot give any legal advice. In addition, every state and even some counties have their own regulations that may be even more stringent than the federal laws. Be careful and ask questions before taking any drastic measures. Regulations are mentioned here to explain the boundaries and overlaps of ergonomics with other programs with which you may already be familiar. This book will not cover all the nuances of every regulation.

For example, most HR professionals are fairly comfortable with the principles of the Americans with Disabilities Act (ADA) and its subsequent revisions. For clarity, I am going to refer to this group of rules as "accommodation regulations" and recommend that you discuss with an attorney or ADA specialist particular differences in the revisions and newer legislation. These regulations and recommendations protect employees from discrimination surrounding disability. The U.S. Equal Employment Opportunity Commission (EEOC) is the entity that gets involved in protecting employees' rights as related to accommodation regulations. The EEOC and the various accommodation regulations protect qualified individuals from being discriminated against during the hiring and promotion process. As a result of these laws, we in the industry got a definition of what it meant to have a "disability."

A person has a disability if she or he has a physical or mental impairment that limits substantially one or more major life activities. The substantial limitation of major life activities refers to impairments that affect seeing, hearing, speaking, walking, breathing, caring for oneself, and working. This disability has to be recorded in some way, usually in some sort of medical documentation. These disabilities are long-term and chronic. Non-chronic conditions or conditions that are of short duration are not generally covered under the accommodation regulations.

These regulations do cover people who have disabilities that are episodic (note this is different from short-term). An example of an episodic disability is seen with multiple sclerosis, where the limitations to function may actually come and go or get worse and get better. It is common with certain types of multiple sclerosis for someone's vision, for example, to get better and worse depending on other factors such as temperature and fatigue. Those changes of vision are covered under the accommodation regulations because this is a known and disclosed disability, even though the person is not disabled all the time.

The complexity of the accommodation regulations is one of the reasons I recommend that you have two separate policies: an ergonomics policy and an accommodations policy. An accommodations policy addresses what you are going to do if you receive medical documentation related to an employee having an injury or reporting a disability. This provides guidance on managing individual concerns. Ergonomics will still be part of the solution; however, it is used with individual needs instead of broad standards. An accommodations policy provides a roadmap when an employee requests a modification to their workspace or work tasks based on a doctor's recommendation or their own stated needs. It gives you a very clear path on how you are going to deal with medical documents, conversations with the employee, and options and opportunities for accommodations. It also gives you a basis for discussing with management the financial ramifications of some potential accommodations. For example, are you going to put requests for sit/stand tables under the heading of accommodations or just a furniture purchase? Will prescription protective eyewear fall under accommodations or supply budgets?

In other words:

You need the **ergonomics policy** for safety, comfort, and health of the masses.

You need the **accommodations policy** for dealing with medical notes and disclosed disabilities for individuals.

Before creating your accommodations policy, it is important to note what the accommodation regulations require of all employers, and what it doesn't. First, the regulations presume that you are dealing with an employee who is qualified to do the job and has a record of a disability or substantial impairment as we defined above.

Your accommodations policy also needs to take into account job tasks that are **essential functions**. These are tasks, behaviors, locations, or methods that are non-negotiable and must exist for the job to be completed. For example, an essential function of a driver is the ability to safely operate a motor vehicle. If the person cannot operate a vehicle, they can't do the job. It is not essential, however, that the job of driver be done using the accelerator and brake pedals with the right foot. If the person can pass a driving test using the left foot, you could not call using the right foot "essential." This may seem like diving too deeply into minutiae. However, these details have come up in courts in the past. Employers have lost cases because they could not justify why a particular task was essential and why inability to do that task was grounds for losing a job. We will discuss accurate and functional job descriptions a bit more in the industrial section, but consider ergonomics, and the detailed analyses that are completed during risk identification, as good tools for teasing out what are essential functions of a job.

The wording of regulations also qualifies the word "accommodation" so as to somewhat protect employers from extravagant requests. It modifies the term with the word "reasonable" in order to assure that the employer is able to have some say in what they can afford and or what their building or structure can be modified to do.

The most important part about the accommodation regulations that many employers forget or ignore is that the regulations do not allow the employee to simply dictate a product needed or state that the employer must give employees specific products. Instead, the regulations open a conversation between the employee and employer regarding what the concept of reasonable means in the individual case. Many times, the employee herself may not know what the best solution is, especially if the disability has become worse or if this is a new job. For example, we have worked with people who know what accommodations they needed to get through their previous job or their schooling. Those accommodations may or may not be appropriate in their new work environment.

It is important to note that the regulations support an interactive process. This interactive process includes an analysis of the job, analysis of what is truly essential for that job, consultation with the individual who is having the problem, and consultation with experts. The final decision should be what is most appropriate for both parties. Therefore, both parties—employee and employer—have a responsibility and a role to play.

Case example:

We worked with a company that had a new employee, we will call him Zack, who was coming directly out of school. Zack had accommodations in school that included a note taker and a reading device that would read written documents out loud. When he arrived at his new job, Zack requested a note taker as an accommodation during group meetings, since he would be attending meetings frequently. An important factor taken into consideration during the accommodation conversation was that the contents of meetings were routinely documented in meeting minutes for everyone's use. An electronic reader was provided to Zack. However, the company questioned whether Zack needed another person to take notes specifically for him during meetings. Zack was asked to first experience a meeting, examine the minutes with his electronic reader, listen to the recording, and evaluate his own ability to recall the events of the meeting before deciding what he needed as an accommodation. After this exercise, Zack found that he did not need any additional notes. He was able to keep up with writing his own notes using a portable braille note-taking device. Instead of paying for an extra note taker or asking one of the staff members to accept that role on top of their own, the company instead covered the cost of a portable braille note-taking device and the brief services of someone to train Zack on efficient use of that device.

This example emphasizes how the regulations exist to open a fair and equitable conversation between the employer and employee. The important step that the company in the above example took -- one which should never, ever be skipped -- was to have a conversation with the employee detailing the nature of the disability and how it may affect the employee's ability to complete the essential functions of the job. Never assume that because you see someone in a wheelchair or you see someone using a white cane that you know what their limitations are.

I have found HR professionals to be very comfortable with the concept of accommodating for a disability disclosed during the hiring process. Most HR professionals understand the concept that you can't deny someone who is fully qualified the chance to work for you just because the applicant discloses a disability.

While the regulations are clear about disabilities, the process is a bit more convoluted and not well-understood regarding how to deal with chronic conditions related to repetitive strain injuries disclosed after the person has been at work. We are not referring here to the worker who fits into the category of "return to work" accommodations. We are talking about workers who may never have left the job and continue to do their jobs without reduction in participation. In general, the regulators have decided that, if someone has WRMSD and informs you, as the employer, they are in essence claiming a condition that may be related to a disability and, therefore, is covered under accommodation rules. Whether accommodations would be required under the regulations depends on whether they can show that the condition significantly affects their ability to participate in major life activities. You need to remember that the HR professional cannot determine whether the person is telling the truth about a disability. The regulations do offer the opportunity to request medical information to clarify the condition or effects of the condition.

Take a moment to look in your HR manual. Do you have an accommodations policy? Does it help you decide how to act and react should you receive notice from an employee about a difficulty at work? Have you defined what will be required from the employee? What will be provided by you? If not, then you are simply working on the basis of "of course we will accommodate a request related to disability because that is the law." Without a policy, you are setting yourself up for trouble later. A protocol is always better than a well meant intention.

What Do I Do When I get a Doctor's Note?

This brings us to one of the reasons a consulting firm such as my own is often brought into another company, and it's a complaint I'm hearing more and more often from the HR community. That is, employees are bringing in prescriptions from physicians stating that they need XYZ piece of equipment, and management does not know what they are supposed to do. If you already have an ergonomics program and an accommodations program, this is not a very scary thing. However, if you don't have them, it is extremely troubling. What are you supposed to do with a doctor's prescription? This is where the worlds of ergonomics and accommodations collide, where you ask yourself whether this an ergonomics request for equipment or rather an accommodations request? Many HR professionals are justifiably concerned that if they don't follow the doctor's prescription, they will be running afoul of the regulations.

Let me put this out there: Doctors' ethics do not allow them to write prescriptions for equipment when they do not know the full effects and side effects, as well as interaction effects, of these items. In other words, you would hope that your doctor would only write prescriptions for medications to treat your arthritis or ulcer. These are diseases or conditions for which he or she has a good understanding of how a specific drug would affect you or interact with any other medications or symptoms you may have. The doctor knows how you should take the drug; e.g., twice a day, once a day. The doctor should be able to advise you on side effects of the treatment and methods to mitigate the side effects.

Well, doctors can't do that for work-related equipment. Strangely though, doctors seem to be getting into some really sticky areas when it comes to equipment, especially for the office. Doctors are routinely telling companies that their patients need a new chair or need to have a standing desk or even a certain mouse. I have even seen doctors sign off on specific chairs (one time it was even a brand that the doctor had stock in—which is a serious ethical issue).

The reality is that there is no way for a doctor who has never been to your site, never seen that workspace, and never observed that employee working, to understand the full scope of the problem or understand the effects of the equipment they have prescribed. You are not a pharmacy and are not required to fill a prescription. However, this does not mean that you should just ignore the prescription and say you don't have to deal with it. Consider it your warning signal. And quite frankly, consider it a late warning signal, since you have already lost money and productivity. The employee is saying "this hurts" or "I can't do this anymore." The doctor's note could be considered as a method of notifying employers of a disability. However, I would encourage you to remember what the accommodation regulations require. The regulations require a conversation and discussion about what is reasonable. I recommend that you include in your ergonomics or accommodations policy a statement that clarifies what will happen when a request for accommodation occurs or a doctor's note is received. If you have an expert on accommodations available to you, please utilize those services. You can state in your policy that you take doctors' recommendations very seriously and that a doctor's note will immediately trigger an evaluation of the work or workspace for potential accommodations. Very often this will solve the problem.

The ergonomic assessment provided by your expert should never include medically confidential information that is inappropriate to keep with your HR files. Whatever wording or phrasing the individual used to request an assessment should be used on that report. If you receive a report from an ergonomics evaluation that states that a person has a disability or has a diagnosis, and that disability or diagnosis was not reported by the employee, I recommend that you return the report to the expert and request a redaction of that information. However, you most likely know even better than I do what medical information should and should not be in your human resources files. The reason for the ergonomics evaluation can be something purposefully vague; for example, "the person reports discomfort in the following area...." Once the report states that there is a pain, this starts crossing the line of medical information and diagnoses, and I would recommend caution in storing these with your HR data. Some companies choose to store ergonomics evaluations with the safety department, medical department, or facilities department in order to get around the suggestion that someone's request for an ergonomics assessment could negatively impact their employment.

The tricky part of the ergonomics/accommodation conversation comes when the expert says that the device or equipment listed in the doctor's note is not actually necessary and the employee really wants one. For example, the doctor's note may say that that person needs a new chair. Your expert comes and assesses the person's current chair and finds that, once its settings are adjusted, the current chair works fine for that individual. If that individual has in mind that they are going to get a new chair and they are not given a new chair, the conversation must continue past this point. The doctor can be requested to state what the person's limitations or restrictions are, and to explain why that person needs a new chair. The employee can be encouraged to discuss with their doctor why a new chair is necessary. At this point, very often a doctor will step back and rescind their request for a new chair. Instead, he will request additional ergonomics services or accommodation evaluations.

Alternatively, doctors can come back with a specific statement that reads something along the lines of: "The person needs a chair that has this feature because of this diagnosis." For example, I have had doctors come back saying the person needs a chair with a headrest because of neck issues. It is highly debatable as to whether headrests have any benefit for specific problems since the computer work environment is so complex. However, once a doctor specifies that the person has a disability related to head control, you as the employer will need to work with the employee and an expert to identify a chair that has that feature. It is unlikely that the legislative bodies will allow you to say that getting a new chair is not reasonable. They do not, however, require that you purchase the brand and style chair recommended by the doctor, unless the doctor can state why the disability requires that specific brand as the accommodation.

At this point, having an expert on your side is a very good thing. The majority of doctors and employees cannot even use specific language to describe equipment. I would challenge any doctor to explain to me what the difference is between the seat pan tilt of a specific chair versus another when I have the specifications in front of me and she doesn't. In fact, it is unlikely that it will get to this point if you have an expert on hand. Later, we will get into what defines an expert so that you can be sure that whoever you use can stand up to scrutiny.

Part 3: How to Design Effective Ergonomics Programs for the Office

Chapter 6: Program Components

The biggest difference between industrial and office ergonomics programs is that office ergonomics programs typically focus immediately on the individual and how that person fits into his or her respective work space. When ergonomics programming is developed for the office, it usually starts after the office has been designed and populated. However, I believe this does a great disservice to your employees. Putting effort into the correct furniture and layout before the space is built-out or furniture purchased is extremely important and makes it possible to fit each individual. Unfortunately, there is limited funding dedicated to including ergonomics in the design of a workplace.

Interior designers usually have some ergonomics knowledge. From talking to quite a number of interior designers, however, I have found that they know they are not ergonomics experts. They are doing their best to make your space aesthetically pleasing while making it flow well. After reading the details that follow of how much is involved in making a space work well for an individual, I hope you will go against the trend of leaving ergonomics out until after design. However, because it is still uncommon for companies to include ergonomics programming as an integral part of office design, this section will focus on more traditional ergonomics programming that assumes the office design has been finished. If you would like more information about how ergonomics is slowly becoming a part of the design process; ergonomics in the green office design movement, or what you should do before your company makes a bulk purchase of equipment, please contact me directly.

Evaluate, Measure, and Report

Within the arena of office ergonomics, there is a wide variety of tools available to help evaluate, measure, and report on risk areas. There are two major groups of evaluations that can be used: those that can be done without an expert and those that require expertise at some level. Some evaluation tools are adapted for portability and remote evaluations, and some still need the evaluator and the employee to be in the same physical space. The reporting component is heavily dependent on the evaluation tool being used, so much so that I have wrapped the documentation component into the evaluation and measurement phase. However, do not underestimate the importance of documenting both the current situation when you begin and what has been done to mitigate risk.

Self-Assessment Ergonomics Tools

If your company will not be working with a trained professional, there are a number of free and for-purchase self-assessment tools online for your employees to use. In fact, there are so many of them I don't have space to list them all and tell you which ones are good and which are not. The features included will depend on what your budget can handle.

I can tell you that free software is typically too simplistic to actually reinforce positive change. Free assessments are very general. The assessments consider issues such as: If the person is sitting in a chair, are their knees where they're supposed to be? Are they sitting up or sitting forward? Free software will usually give broad recommendations such as "sit back in the chair," "raise the armrests," "move your monitor forward," or "try a different mouse." These recommendations don't necessarily help your employees, because often they are geared towards a simple ergonomics fix such as, "If your chair doesn't fit, buy a new one" or "If your arms hurt, get a new keyboard." And as we previously explained, the overly simple fixes do not actually solve the problem.

However, if a free assessment is all that you can afford, OSHA provides a fairly thorough assessment online that includes some guidelines on how to correct problems identified. The assessment is a simplified checklist of whether a certain situation is present or not (yes/no). This is what the first part of the OSHA tool looks like in electronic form:

https://www.osha.gov/SLTC/etools/computerworkstations/checklist_evaluation.html

The OSHA tool also includes a buying guide for solutions to some of the problems that may be noted in the assessment. This is very important in assisting the user in finding solutions.

On the other hand, many of the more expensive self-assessment tools and programs are highly customizable and detailed. They work with a much more complex decision tree to figure out appropriate recommendations. I've worked with a few of the more detailed self-assessment tools to modify them for the equipment relevant to a particular employer. This does take time and a budget. More customizable software can be integrated with other components, such as stretch break software or educational videos. You can add or subtract based on what your expert has told you works for your workforce.

Professional Assessments: Individual

If your company has decided to work with an ergonomics professional or paraprofessional, the next service to add to ergonomic programs is typically individual assessments. Individual assessments can be done by an expert or someone trained by the expert to provide one-on-one assessment and education. The individual assessment addresses an immediate problem, hopefully in a relatively quick time period. As we discussed in program design, assessments are usually first provided to people who have complained of problems or have filed worker's compensation complaints. The reactive ergonomic assessments include an individual assessment and a very detailed individual report. With most ergonomics programs, the rest of the staff will be provided services only after the priority staff, that is, those with complaints, have been evaluated. After everyone with pressing issues has been dealt with, staff members who fit into the category of rapid response and preventative services receive evaluations. Typically, the pacing of assessments has to do with budget and scaling up of the ergonomics program. One-on-one detailed assessments are more costly than the preventative or rapid response shortened version. The detailed assessment of someone who already has a problem just takes more time.

One of the concerns that HR managers have expressed to me is that, if they offer ergonomic services to one person, they will have to offer it to everyone. Or, if they offer evaluations to one person, suddenly everyone will say they have a problem. The concern is grounded in facts—I cannot fault you on that one. Think of it this way--at first the program will reach only part of the staff and probably carry a higher per-person price tag. As people hear about the ergonomics program, you will see a spike in requests. You have a few choices at this point to control the flow of evaluations and control your immediate expense:

- Tell your staff that they need a doctor's note or must have some specific problem to be scheduled to see an ergonomics expert. The result is a very expensive program on both the healthcare and ergonomics fronts, and expenses continue to be high for a long period because all assessments are done reactively.

- Tell your staff that anyone can get an individual assessment by request. The result is also expensive for a long period, but you get rid of the doctor's visit because all assessments are done one-on-one as if there is a stated problem. The assessments are still the detailed type.

- Initiate a group approach to allow anyone who wants an assessment to have a brief assessment as part of a walk-through (details to follow) or attend a class with small-group assistance. The result is a program that is a lot less expensive per person with rapidly decreasing costs because the assessments take less time per person, even when each person is seen one-on-one. The assumption is that there is no stated problem that needs to be accommodated.

Most ergonomics companies create their own assessment format and documentation. The customized and proprietary assessments are more detailed and often document changes that are made during the assessment process. The ergonomics company may have assigned risk levels based on that company's experience with various computer work station issues; however, there is no one gold standard of assessing severity of risk.

- The in-person reactive individual assessment typically follows this pattern:

- The reason for the assessment is gathered using an interview.

- Work habits such as time spent at the computer are documented.

- Photographs are taken of the workstation prior to any changes being made.

- Measurements are taken, if needed, of the position of equipment relative to either the floor or desk.

- Notations are made regarding the issues seen that are moving the employee out of neutral posture, such as the chair being too big or the monitor too high.

- Most assessments include time to make changes to the workstation in order to address any pressing concerns within the confines of available equipment; for example, adjusting the chair to better fit the person or raising the monitor height.

- Notations are made regarding any additional equipment that may be needed or is recommended based on the assessment. ¶

¶ - *It is important to note that you as the employer have control over how much is discussed regarding equipment with the employee at the time of the evaluation; you just have to let the evaluator know your decision beforehand. Some employers request that the evaluator not discuss equipment recommendations at all with the employee since the final decision of what is purchased will be made later through a different avenue. Some employers request that the evaluator only discuss equipment options from a pre-approved equipment list. And some employers allow the evaluator to discuss any equipment with the employee with the understanding that budgeting may need to be considered.*

It also is important to note that the employee must be present at the time of the evaluation. Regardless of whether this is an evaluation done in a group or individually, an office ergonomics evaluation is always centered around setting up a workstation for a specific person. If the workstation is shared by multiple people, then it is useful for all employees who share that workstation to be present.

- Photographs are taken to document any changes made, including changes to the person's posture.

Office assessments typically include time to make physical changes to the workstation. Even if the changes that were made were equipment focused, it is difficult for employees to maintain the new postures without reinforcement. Usually, people fall back into bad habits such as slouching or resting their wrists while keying. It is important for office programs to include follow-up to not only ensure that the solution presented solved the problem, but to verify that people are still following the recommended actions—reminders are needed! These reminders could take the form of an electronic self-assessment reminding people to pay attention to their own behaviors. A regular walkthrough with brief assessments to remind people of proper set-ups is greatly effective. Reminder programs, which will be discussed in detail later, play a large role in creating lasting change.

Professional Assessments: For the Masses

Once individuals with specific and pressing problems have been managed, the next component to be added is preventative or rapid response group assessments. This approach usually includes some form of short worksite assessments completed for a large number of employees all in one sweep. The interview process is shorter. Measurements of the workstation are not taken unless very specific to the recommendations. The assessments are typically shorter in duration overall than a reactive assessment and may have a briefer reporting system.

The group approach is typically used with companies that have decided to take a more proactive stance but do not yet have the capability of being truly proactive. Let me explain the difference. A truly proactive program will have assessments done prior to the person starting work and then on a regular basis, whether or not there has been the complaint of a problem. The phase discussed here, assessing large groups at once, which we call "worksite walk-throughs," is usually done on a voluntary basis—someone signs up for the assessment. The ergonomics evaluator gets a list of people who are interested in getting an assessment and then goes person-to-person in a fairly rapid fashion to help each set up his or her workstation. The evaluator logs any changes that are necessary or makes changes that are readily available. We have found that the people who sign up for assessments typically have some form of discomfort, but have not yet reached the point of visiting a medical professional, or they have seen a medical professional but have not reported specific problems to their employer. Over the many years we've been doing this work, we've found the majority of employees evaluated have had some experience with discomfort, especially when the company is first instituting these worksite walk-throughs. This pre-existing discomfort is why I do not describe these worksite walk-throughs as purely preventative.

As the ergonomics program matures and more people have been seen using these worksite walk-throughs, the trend then moves to one of a more preventative nature. Employees are seen during the on-boarding process, before starting work. Additionally, an employee who may have been evaluated because they were having some form of discomfort is seen a year later because they need only a refresher.

Addressing the Problems: What Does an Office Ergonomics Assessment Look Like?

Example: Jodi and Her Arm Pain

Returning to our employee Jodi, let's look at an example of what we often see in an office environment and how ergonomics would help solve the problems.

As we discussed earlier, our employee, Jodi, has requested an ergonomic assessment because she is having discomfort in her arms. During the assessment, she is found to be sitting at her desk perched at the edge of her chair, reaching forward for her keyboard and mouse. She looks something like this (see fig L):

Figure L: Jodi before changes are made

Think back to our idea of stability and then mobility. In order to address her arm pain, we must first assess her base of support. To give you some idea of how this is done, let's start from the bottom and work our way up, just as we would do in an assessment. [6]

First, her **feet** need to be supported. To accomplish this, either the chair has to be lowered or her feet put up on a footrest.

Figure M: Two options for supporting Jodi's feet

6- This is going to be a very brief description; you should not expect to be able to do a full office ergonomics assessment just by reading it. I have an entire book on how to do an ergonomics assessment if you would like to take that route. Think of this as getting us all on the same path before moving onto the nitty-gritty.

Now that we have her feet supported, look at the seat pan, or the part of the chair her buttocks rest on. Is it small enough so that it is not pushing into the back of her legs when she is sitting all the way back in the chair? Is it large enough to support most of her leg? Or is it creating pressure areas on the backs of her thighs? Depending on the answers to these questions, the chair may need to be adjusted, modified, or adapted to better fit her leg length.

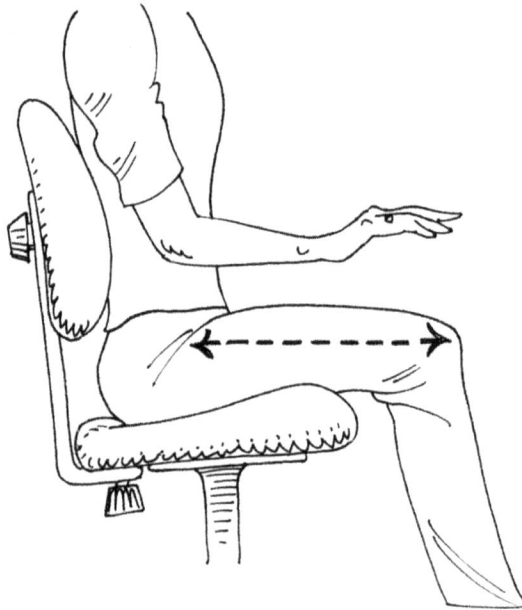

Figure N: Seat pan length

Next, let's move up her **spine**. Is she sitting upright but supported? When she relaxes her core musculature, does she slide down and drop her ribs into her pelvis? The chair will need to be adjusted so that the curvature of the backrest matches the curvature of her spine in height and depth. This will take some trial and error. Have her sit back against the backrest and relax between each trial. Watch her spine and posture. She should be able to sit back against the backrest while still maintaining an upright posture.

Figure O: Sliding out of chair versus sitting upright

Move the assessment out to her **arms**. Check her armrests. Do they interfere with her arm movements or keep her from putting her elbows against her ribs (neutral posture)? There is great debate in the world of seated postures regarding whether a person's arms should be externally supported while typing.[21] The research is inconclusive, most likely because there are so many factors affecting arm position, including but certainly not limited to:

- Overall posture of the back, neck and shoulders

- What the person is doing with her arms while seated

- Any reaching needed

Figure P: Armrests interfering (aka, Armrests gone wrong)

Only now that she has a good base of support can we address the tools she is using, namely the computer. It is important to address the location of each component: **keyboard, mouse, and any other externals.** Remember the reach envelope. If she regularly has to reach outside of her primary reach envelope so as to reach the keyboard and mouse, she will be destabilizing herself. Her body weight is pulling her forward and down— gravity always wins. By moving the keyboard and mouse close to her, we place her weight back against the backrest and reduce the likelihood that she will slump forward.

Since it is brought up frequently, let's discuss **wrist rests.** The primary purposes of wrist rests are to reduce the likelihood of pressure areas against a sharp desk edge and/or to provide support for the arms. Scan back a few paragraphs and consider why Jodi may have pressure on her wrists while typing or using the mouse. Either the desk is too high and her wrists have to be protected from the desk edge, or she is reaching out and has to support the weight of her arms. Again, there is no good research out there about wrist rests being definitively good or bad.[22] Considering the multiple variables involved, this is not surprising. Instead of relying on rules to make the decision for your employee, use the concepts above to reduce the likelihood of injuries occurring due to the use or non-use of a wrist rest.

Don't forget that the **monitor** is also a tool and can directly affect posture and visual strain. The visual distance to read the screen can be considered her visual envelope. Jodi wears progressive lenses and has to move her head out of a neutral position to see the screen. She tends to jut her chin forward and look down her nose in an attempt to look at the monitor through her reading lenses.

Figure Q: When the chin juts forward to see the screen because of glasses

First, we must adjust the height of the monitor so that she can look through the middle part of her lenses, that is, the area set for middle distances. Next, we have to set the screen at an appropriate distance from her eyes so that she can see it easily without craning her neck.

Put all together, the changes listed above will make her look like this (see fig R):

Figure R: After changes are made to her workstation

Here, she has a good base of support that is promoting an upright and supportive spinal alignment. Her work tools are set to reduce strain and assist her in maintaining proper posture.

From this example, ergonomics for the office looks relatively easy on the surface—just make everyone look like this. Unfortunately, not everyone thrives in this position, so I can't really simplify it to a formulaic position; this is just a sample position that works well. So, why do office ergonomics programs cause such concerns for HR professionals? When you were reading the section above, did dollar signs start running around your head? How much will it be to put something under her feet? What if she needs a new chair? What if this doesn't solve the problems??

If an evaluation is done incorrectly, yes, you can end up paying a lot to solve a "simple" problem. If an evaluation is done by someone who gets their paycheck by selling equipment to you, yes, you can end up paying a lot of money. It is important for you to understand what needs to be assessed so that when you are talking to prospective experts, you will know what to listen for.

Chapter 7: Training

If an employee is not educated in how to make changes to his or her workplace, or education is not part of an ergonomics evaluation, there is the option to address ergonomics corrections through group training. Many companies chose to start an ergonomics program with training due to budget constraints. By no means do I want you to consider training as something that should be skipped if your company cannot provide individual evaluations. Training is also a good method to reinforce behavior change, proper equipment use, and postural changes made during an assessment. Training can take on many forms, so I am presenting a few of the many options for training here, along with some notes on how well each type of training works.

Health Fairs

Health fairs are a low-cost option, as many doctors' offices or physical or occupational therapy offices are willing to provide ergonomics education services for free or at very low cost. A word of warning: You get what you pay for. Some of the therapists and doctors who provide ergonomics education at health fairs for free often do not practice ergonomics and are regurgitating what is found on the internet or was taught to them in school some years ago. Now, just to be clear, I am not saying that all therapists and doctors who provide educational services for free are incompetent! Just that they have an ulterior motive for providing free services at your health fair — it may be a marketing strategy to get your employees into their clinics.

An additional problem with health fairs is that your employees do not learn ergonomics well from visiting a booth at a health fair. The changes that need to be done to the workstation are too physical in nature. Health fairs or wellness fairs are very good at showing your employees what resources are available. When it comes to ergonomics, very often a company does not make additional resources available after the health fair, so then what are you telling your employees?

My company no longer will participate in fairs for companies that do not have and are not considering some type of ergonomics program. We provide basic information in small bites so that people walking through the fair can at least take *something* away. Unfortunately, if we don't already work with that company, we have no way of providing more information or follow up. We have, in essence, whetted the employees' appetites and left them wanting. That doesn't mean a health fair is bad; it just means that I would like for you to consider it a starting point. Perhaps consider it an opening event to get an idea of what types of problems you have. A fair will help bring to your attention some information about how many people would like help later on.

Health fairs are wonderful places to get your employees thinking about their cholesterol or their dental health because these are services provided by other companies and you are simply the connector between the employee and provider. If you are not ready to deal with the employees who come to you for more ergonomics help, then I recommend caution when including ergonomics presentations at a health fair. You as the employer need to maintain control of ergonomics experts that come into your company. You do not want employees to take the information provided at the health fair and use it as a springboard to look for additional ergonomics services on their own.

Lunch and Learns

One basic component found in many ergonomics programs is a "lunch and learn," or a short educational program that fits in during a lunch or snack break. In other words, a workshop that brings your employees together in a room where someone presents a lecture. This is a very useful tool in that it reaches a large number of people for a very small amount of money; however, it is also the tool that provides the least results.

First, this type of education is usually provided by professionals or paraprofessionals who are providing the education as a means of marketing their services. Just as in the health fair discussion above, many who provide free or very low-cost lunch and learns have not taken the time to get continuing education past what they learned in school or from the internet. I recommend caution when bringing someone in who has no knowledge of your company and your equipment. Unfortunately, the person giving the lunch and learn will have to provide your employees some very generalized solutions. The educator may very well mention equipment that you have no intention of buying or that would not be effective in your workplace.

Second, as with health fairs, the common complaint after a lunch and learn is that more problems or more requests for equipment occur after the lunch and learn than before. Understand that by giving a lunch and learn, you have opened the door of communication. This is a very good thing, but be prepared for the response. If you do nothing else, please do lunch and learns. However, be ready to deal with additional requests for services or equipment afterward.

Educational Videos

Educational videos are very common in office ergonomics and are very inexpensive because the company does not need to pay an instructor for each class completed. Videos, however, fall under two broad categories: generic and customized, with each providing very different results. The generic videos show someone using a generic chair, computer, monitor, and mouse to help your employees understand how to set up their workstations. The worst plan you could use is a generic video shown to the employee when the employee is away from his desk. The likelihood of a video shown without context leading to true change is slim to none.

If the generic video is available to the employee while she is sitting at her workstation, there is some possibility that positive change can occur. With this plan, you rely on the employee to be able to determine where their own body parts are in relation to equipment—equipment that they don't necessarily know how to use. The inability to understand how to use specific pieces of equipment and to internalize physical movement revisions limits the effectiveness of videos in general and generic videos specifically. The majority of your employees do not know where their bodies are in space. While this may seem ludicrous, think about the amount of time a professional dancer spends in front of a mirror. Even a professional dancer cannot correctly identify specific body part positions and postures without external cues. An employee who has been positioned at the same work space for many years most definitely cannot internally determine the correctness of their own posture without assistance. However, employees can at least get a little better if they can experience the education in context at their desks.

Figure S: Can we really see ourselves?

Custom videos are typically made using your company's equipment in your environment, and include detailed instructions on how to use your equipment.

The nice thing about a customized video is that when a person sees on the video, "Use this lever" on the chair, he can find that lever on his chair. The employee is not hearing "use this lever if you could possibly find it on your multiple variable chairs." Of all of the video types, the customized videos tend to work the best and, not surprisingly, are also expensive. However, customized videos do not have to be very expensive. In many cases, the ergonomics expert can work with a few of your staff members and a handheld video camera or phone to create a video. You also can videotape a workshop when the workshop takes place using your workstations.

Of greatest importance is that the video represents what your employees actually have available. Customized videos typically include instructions and pause points. These are declarative sentences that tell your employees to stop the video and make a change. The pause reduces the likelihood of employees hearing only a part of the message or not being able to recall details after the video has ended. Again, customized videos work best when viewed at the workstation, and don't work as well when viewed in a group workshop location. Customized videos also work well as part of reminder programs and can be sent out after evaluations have been completed.

Computer Software/Apps

When I refer to apps here, it is just to mention that videos, self-assessments, stretch programs, and combination programs are sometimes available in app form so that your employees can take assistance with them on the road. Many of the apps are simplified versions of the more expansive (and expensive) full software versions.

There is a type of app now on the market that allows for remote evaluations and remote training by an ergonomics provider. I've looked at a number of these and so far have not found any that meet all of my clients' requirements. However, they may fit into your budget best, so I feel it is my responsibility to mention them here. Often these apps lead the person through a self-assessment, including places where the person is supposed to take a picture of themselves or have someone take a picture of them, so that a third party can review the picture and self-assessment. The app provider can then send information back to the employee and thereby provide training remotely. I have not been able to get a good sense of how well these are working for other companies and cannot give you a conclusive statement of value. Our company offers something similar to our clients, but we have not put it in app format. I have found that, since we are working with different cultures and different technologies, the app format is not the best solution for our clients. Instead, we use a simple web form or even written instructions for photographs to be sent by email to the expert. Training is then provided remotely via written instructions and webinars.

There are a number of software programs that can integrate self-evaluations, video training, reminders, and stretch breaks. This comprehensive software often includes diagnostic measurement tools to let you know how often employees are taking their breaks, whether employees have done a reassessment, how much employees are actually typing, and whether employees are reporting consistent use of the equipment that you issued. The software also can let you know if employees are skipping the breaks that you've mandated so that there can be some follow-up by supervisors.

This software is expensive; however, I feel that it makes an excellent *companion* to live help. I have yet to see a program that can replace an in-person assessment or live training. In survey after survey, we are seeing people request in-person assistance, even from the groups who are extremely tech savvy. It seems that we continue to be a species that requires in-person, personalized assistance in order to change our behaviors or postures. I have seen people tell me that their elbows are bent and I'm looking right at them seeing that their elbows are straight. We simply have a hard time internalizing and evaluating what we are actually doing. The biggest "aha" moments that my clients have are when we show them their before and after pictures. Many people believe they're not *that bad* until they see the difference for themselves.

Chapter 8: How Do I Help Employees Remember?

As we see with New Year's resolutions, it is very difficult to change old habits. Therefore, a reminder system, a system that keeps ergonomics in the forefront, is needed to ensure that the ergonomics principles demonstrated during the assessment process are not forgotten. The reminder program for the office could be in the form of automated electronic reminders or in-person repeat visits or a combination of these. To have the best effect, reminders need to be frequent, relevant, and systematic. Emails about upcoming ergonomics events will not necessarily be as effective as an email directing employees to take a moment to sit up wherever they may seated.

Break Software

In a simplistic way, break software is designed to distract a person from the job for a brief moment and encourage them to do something else. This something else could be a yoga stretch; it could be a dance move; or it could be deep breathing to relaxing music. A stretch reminder program is a useful and reasonably priced tool. However, unless it is customizable, that is, more expensive, the stretch program will only remind your employees to get up and move regularly. I have modified some programs to alternate stretches with directives to remind employees to apply ergonomics principles, such as "Don't be a turtle," or "Are your arms down by your sides?". If there is no budget for additional software, a similar effect can be accomplished by a repeated meeting programmed into the calendar system. Smart watches, fitness monitoring watches, and phone apps also can provide reminder notifications.

In truth, I've seen people both love and hate reminder programs because they interrupt the work day. I can't give you a good pre-determined barometer to help you decide if it's worth the investment as, interestingly enough, some employees I'd guessed would hate the reminder programs like them, and some I'd thought would like the programs hate them. Since these systems are fairly inexpensive and can be turned off for those people who actually dislike them, I recommend instituting some type of pop-up reminder program when the budget is available.

A word of caution: Some programs are very random regarding the level of expertise needed to complete a stretch. The program does not take into consideration what the person's capabilities may be or give the employee a gentle alternative if the stretch is too difficult. It is also important to select a break program that is appropriate for the culture of the office. For example, if everyone is in business attire, a stretch program that asks employees to get down on the ground and put their legs in the air would not be appropriate. Software that enables you to customize it, even in a very simple on-off manner, is preferable.

Want a playful solution to a tight budget? I worked with a small company that decided that every mid-morning and mid-afternoon, the receptionist would get on the overhead paging system, and play two minutes of a dance song. In another company, I directed a small workgroup to assign someone on the team to be the reminder person. This person would stand up at predetermined times and shout a random word that does not belong in the regular workplace, such as kangaroo or asparagus. This served to break people's concentration long enough to take a short break. It also caused people to start laughing— a wonderful way of achieving healthy blood supply and airflow.

Chapter 9: Develop an Ergonomics Culture

In the majority of work cultures in the United States, we are programmed from a very young age to claim a seat if possible. Many of the games we play as children include some form of winning if you get a seat. We are instructed to sit still and behave, or to sit down and do our homework. This behavior continues into our adulthood with the perception that working hard is synonymous with being seated and that others may perceive us as not paying attention if we are standing or walking.

> I ran an experiment in one of my large public lectures. On the projector screen, I put the following note: "Please find a seat, put your things down on it, and do not sit down unless you need to." Even though I saw a number of people look directly at the screen and read my note, and laugh, the majority of people chose to sit down. I call this behavior "seat-seeking behavior."

This seat-seeking behavior, or constantly looking for a place to sit or lean, is a primary concern. We will get into the sit/stand desk phenomenon in the next section, but consider all of the times people sit down, other than when at the desk. The same people who ask me for a sit/stand desk get onto public transportation and fight for a seat. It is customary to show respect by offering a guest a chair. I have asked people to limit the use of visitors' chairs in the office to guests from outside the company or for truly serious conversations. I have asked employees instead to offer colleagues the opportunity to "take a stand." I'm intrigued by the number of people who insist on a sit/stand desk and then refuse to stand in public transportation, large conferences, or brief meetings. One of the challenges to the creation of a successful ergonomics program is to promote a cultural change to move from a seated focus to a movement focus—a focus that does not require a change of furniture. In other words, your ergonomics program does not need to include a complete refit of all of your equipment. It may, however, need a commitment from the company to promote a cultural change from seat-seeking to movement-celebrating. In some companies, especially where the climate is consistently warm, taking walking meetings outside has become part of the culture.

Moving to Truly Preventative Programs in the Office

Once evaluations of employees with high risk and employees with discomfort are managed, and groups of current employees are being educated regularly, the last phase or component that is added to an office ergonomics program is that of true preventative action. Employees are provided an ergonomics evaluation on their first day of work, during which their workstations are set up correctly. Employees are then seen on a regular basis to ensure that they continue to work correctly and that the workstation is set up properly. These preventative follow-ups usually take only a few minutes and are designed to reinforce good practices and to spot issues before they become problems.

As we have discussed, the general progression of ergonomics programming for office environments is from reactive to rapid response to proactive. How quickly your company moves through that process depends on your budget and key stakeholder buy-in. There are a variety of tools that can be used for each stage of the ergonomics programming with varying costs and effectiveness. Whether you decide to try to save money and provide low-cost or automated tools or chose to spend money on experts, the important fact is that you are addressing the problem.

We already have walked through an evaluation. The next chapter is designed to help you understand some of the physical components of the office space as it relates to ergonomics. The chapter will also cover some of the "alternative" workplaces, as well as non-traditional equipment that has been gaining favor with the media. After discussing the type of equipment available, I will take a moment to do a deep dive into whether or not is it bad to sit.

Chapter 10: The Computer Workstation

The type of equipment that can go into offices has expanded rapidly in the last few years. Some of the demand for this new equipment stems from a myth that has been perpetuated through the internet, and some has basis in reality. To ensure that you are ready for the questions your employees will ask, I will address some of them in this book.

I'll be making an attempt to clarify what equipment is really needed, available, used, or overused in a computer situation. Before I do that, however, I want to point out something that should seem fairly obvious. The majority of the population who work at computers do not actually spend most of their days working on computers. They go to meetings. They run errands. They talk on the phone. They talk to colleagues. In fact, we recently got a chance to informally study how a few hundred people actually worked at their computers. The majority of the people in this project reported that they worked at the computers "all day." They reported they felt like they were "stuck" at their desks.

When we looked at employees' keyboard and mouse use, we found that they were actually working on their computers actively only about 3 to 4 hours per day. We theorized that employees associate working in their office with working on the computer. The results also showed that active professionals were often working other places besides in the office. Employees would take laptops to meetings or on the road. They would use their cell phones or tablets for extended periods of time and not be on the computer at all.

There are a variety of set-ups within an office environment. For example, the offices may have adjustable height desks or keyboard trays; the staff may use two or more monitors; or the staff may need to reference a lot of paper while working on the computer.

> The basic principles of stability and mobility, decreasing reach, and limiting repetition and force should be expanded to cover any office arrangement.

Beyond the Chair and Desk

Some basic and relatively inexpensive components that can be added to a workstation to make it better fit your employees include:

- footrests

- monitor risers

- monitor arms

- keyboard trays

- alternative keyboards or mice

Footrests

Footrests come in a variety of materials, styles, price ranges, and heights. The majority of users require a footrest that adjusts in one of two height ranges: between 2 to 4 inches, which I call **standard footrests,** as the majority of footrests on the market fit this range; or the user will need a footrest that adjusts between 4 to 6 inches, which I call **tall footrests**. I recommend adjustable-height footrests if you can get them. (When employees are in countries that have limited resources, we often will simply have a carpenter make a variety of footrests out of wood in a variety of heights.)

The slope or rocking motion of many footrests helps users find a comfortable angle for the ankle and foot. The slope or angle of the footrest serves two main purposes: It allows people who wear shoes with heels to release their ankles and have their feet flat, that is, a high heel can drop down at the bottom of the slope while the toe is supported at the top; and it allows people to sit with their feet slightly in front of their knees while still feeling like they have good foot support. The footrests that rock can accommodate someone who wears shoes with various heel heights throughout the year or people who fidget. Note that some users really dislike the footrests that rock and some users really love rocking footrests—there is no specific pattern to identify who will like which type. In general, the best course of action is to set a standard of what will be purchased and then accommodate anyone who desperately dislikes the type selected.

The majority of footrests on the market are made out of plastic. Bear in mind that it's important to also have more sturdy, wide metal footrests available for employees who are obese, employees who have broken prior footrests by the tendency to push off of the foot rest when standing up, or employees who sit with a very wide distance between their feet and cannot bring their legs together comfortably (many men sit this way). Conversely, metal footrests also tend to be more difficult to adjust in height, although many do have some adjustability.

If more than six inches of height is needed, a specialized footrest is used. The markets call these footrests **industrial or lab height footrests**. These are the type used with static standing desks. The industrial or lab-height footrests are adjustable to a greater height while still maintaining their stability. The industrial and lab footrests have a corresponding increase in cost, but in many cases are well worth it in value.

Monitor Risers

Monitor risers are basically plastic or metal boxes or shelves that raise the monitor to the correct height. The monitor should be straight ahead of the user, and the top of the screen should be just above the user's eye height. Some monitors come with built-in adjustability in their stands. Even with this built-in adjustability, some employees will need the additional height provided by a monitor riser.

These two very inexpensive items, footrests and monitor risers, are the most common items that evaluators will recommend. The monitor riser and footrest often will solve the problems associated with a chair not feeling comfortable. Later in this chapter, we will review chair components and making a chair fit, but the most common reason that people complain of back pain or neck pain is because their feet are not on the floor or not supported. So instead of a $600 chair, the problem can be addressed with around $60 worth of equipment in the form of a footrest and monitor riser. The prevalent need for footrests and monitor risers is the reason I warn companies ahead of time that I am going to use up all available reams of paper when doing evaluations for large groups. Reams of paper are very handy for temporarily supporting feet and raising monitors *and* provide a demonstration of what height support is needed for each employee.

Monitor Arms

A more complex variation on monitor risers are monitor arms. Monitor arms are adjustable rods that clamp or screw into the desk and to the monitor. Monitor arms allow the position and the height of the monitor to be changed easily. Monitor arms come in a variety of designs that each have their positives and negatives. When deciding whether to use a monitor arm, you should be aware of these factors: the depth of the desk, the number of monitors that need to be supported, and whether the monitors need to be mobile.

If an employee is sitting at a static sitting or static standing desk, adjustments to the monitor may be possible using the less expensive monitor riser. If the employee is at an adjustable or sit/stand desk, the mobility of a monitor arm would be preferable to allow for additional adjustability. The higher cost of monitor arms will need to be taken into account when budgeting for sit/stand or adjustable desks.

An additional consideration for selecting a monitor arm is how many monitors the employee uses. While there are dual and triple monitor arm units available, I do not typically recommend using them because there are limitations to how each monitor can be arranged when they are all attached to the same arm. For example, if you use multiple large-screen monitors, the adjustability of the monitor arms becomes limited by the monitors overlapping in certain positions. Multiple single monitor arm units can be purchased at prices similar to one dual or triple monitor arm unit when purchased in bulk. If the work station will be used by multiple employees, it is important to use multiple single monitor arms to accommodate employees with different visual acuity. It is also important to understand how far forward the monitor arms reach on a desk. If you have very deep desks, such as oversized wooden executive styles, the monitor arm needs to be able to bring the monitor within 18 inches of the front of the desk. To achieve this reach, you may have to purchase longer monitor arms or drill into the desk surface.

Case example:

We recently completed evaluations for an office where all employees used more than one monitor. Two employees in particular had complaints regarding not being able to see the monitors correctly. One employee used reading glasses and one employee had perfect vision. Both worked in cubicles with dual monitor arms. The employee who used reading glasses was unable to pull the monitors close enough because the monitors would start to overlap as they got closer. The employee who had perfect vision was unable to push the monitors away far enough to be comfortable. As the monitors were pushed away the monitors separated and the person was stuck looking far to the right and far to the left for each monitor. This situation would not have occurred if the office was using two single monitor arms instead of one dual monitor arm.

Keyboard Trays

Keyboard trays come in a myriad of designs, controls, and styles. It is important to note that both the keyboard and the mouse need to be on the keyboard tray to allow for proper positioning of the user's arms. Avoid keyboard trays that do not have sufficient space for both keyboard and mouse. [††] While it would be beyond the scope of this book to go through each and every keyboard tray available, there are a few features that I would recommend taking into account:

Static versus adjustable keyboard trays:

There are keyboard and mouse trays on the market that are called "trays," but should be called "drawers." These are keyboard and mouse trays that are not adjustable in height or tilt and sometimes can't be slid under the desk. While static drawers are less expensive, I recommend caution when considering these units because your long-term ability to use them for multiple people is limited. However, static trays are an inexpensive option that does bring the keyboard and mouse lower than the desk surface.

Adjustable keyboard trays raise and lower relative to the user, tilt forwards and backwards, and sometimes slide under the desk. Each brand of keyboard tray has different mechanisms to accomplish the adjustability features. A word of caution: It is been my experience that employees do not like the mechanisms that use an adjustment tool or knob that sticks out from the side of the keyboard tray because it hits users on the knee. It is not comfortable to be working at your desk with something constantly pressing into your knee. I recommend you look at units that say "tilt-to-adjust." In order to adjust these trays, you lift the front of the tray and push down on the back of the tray to raise and lower the tray itself; there are no mechanical parts jutting from the side of the tray.

Slide or Track Depth:

Before you purchase a tray, it is important to decide how much depth is available on the desk to allow this tray to fully retract when not in use. The keyboard tray

---

†† - Note: *The name of the tray does not typically differ if the tray has room for a mouse or does not—they are all called "keyboard trays."*

moves forward and backwards on something called a "slide" or "track." The slides usually come in two standard lengths of 19 inches or 21 inches. Measure the depth of the underside of the desk from the front edge to the back edge and ensure that the area is free from protuberances.

Desk Arrangements: Four Categories

There are a number of options and a number of different terminologies for desk arrangements. They can roughly be broken into four categories:

- static
- adjustable
- retrofit
- replacement

Each of these have various pros and cons and, in reality, different uses. In order to understand how each type of desk fits into the ergonomics equation, let me define these four categories.

Static Desk

A static desk by definition can be a static sitting desk or a static standing desk. A static sitting desk is the desk that most of us think about when we think of the term "desk." These are work surfaces that are approximately 29 to 30 inches above the floor and do not adjust. This style of work surface has been in use for a very long time and was initially designed for people who used paper.

To make a static sitting desk fit the majority of the population, as you saw in the example of Jodi, the employee has to be raised in her chair so that the desk is at the same level as her elbow when she is seated. Alternatively, the employee can be lowered in the chair so that her feet are supported on the floor. In this situation, the keyboard will then need to be brought down using a keyboard tray of some type).

Figure T: Two options for corrected sitting at a static desk

Once the idea of standing work got attention in the media, a trend started of people installing counter-height desks that did not adjust and calling those "standing desks." These standing desks vary widely in installation height, but are most commonly set at around 45 to 48 inches from the floor. When these standing desks are installed, the assumption is that a computer workstation will be put on top of that surface. I have seen many difficulties with this arrangement. The height selected, whatever that might be, rarely fits the employees who have to use the desks. Most employees require additional equipment to be installed on these standing desks to make them usable as computer workstations. This defeats the whole purpose of the original installation. It is unlikely that a short employee would be able to stand safely on a step in order to lower the static *standing* desk relative to the elbow height. Therefore, the keyboard and mouse must be brought down to the employee by installing a keyboard tray of some type.

Regardless of whether employees use a static sitting desk or a static standing desk, opportunities need to be given to work in the alternate position. If the person uses the computer at a static sitting desk, he needs ample opportunities to stand throughout the day. The person can stand while working on paperwork or talking on the phone and could also stand while having informal meetings.

The reverse is true when someone has a static standing desk. Employees need to be given opportunities to sit down, such as during informal meetings, while doing paperwork, or when on the phone. It is important to note that people typically cannot tolerate static standing for more than 5 to 30 minutes at a time. They have to either start walking around or shift position or sit down. If someone who is standing is not given the opportunity to sit down, posture degenerates and the person starts to hang off the desk or stand in awkward postures.

Figure U: Poor posture at standing desk

To integrate enough sitting into the day, static standing desks need to have the capability of being used seated or the user needs another work space available in order to work seated. If the user will be seated at a static standing height desk, he will also need to have a tall working chair and a tall foot rest. The seated posture does not change from a regular seated desk; the footrest and chair just get taller. The added chair and footrest is an expense very often neglected. In other words, we have simply replaced one problem with another—now people are standing too much.

Adjustable Height Desks

Adjustable height desks are desks that are designed to allow different seated heights. When desks are referred to as "adjustable height desks," it often means that the desk does not have a wide enough height range to adjust it for both sitting and standing. Also, adjustable desks often do not have a gear or handle mechanism designed to allow for easy and frequent height adjustments. Instead, these desks use manual cranks or locking pins for height adjustability. It is important to distinguish between adjustable height desks and sit/stand desks. They are not the same. Even adjustable height desks that will go up high enough for standing are not typically used for a true sit/stand protocol since they are not easily adjusted and it is impractical to change the height with any regularity. When ordering adjustable height desks, it is important to look at the lowest end of the heights available. It is best to use adjustable height desks that lower to around the 24 or 25 inch height range. With a desk at around 24 to 25 inches, you will be able to fit the majority of your employees with the proper seated keyboard height. An easy way to think about how low a desk needs to go is that keyboard height, and therefore desk surface height if not using a keyboard tray, is determined by the height of the person's elbow or lap when sitting properly in a chair with their feet supported on the ground. An easy way to determine what that height of a desk should be is to measure the height of the person's kneecap.

However, the American population does not particularly like to sit that low relative to the ground and the people surrounding them. It feels uncomfortable. From a sociocultural standpoint, it puts the person below what is considered a natural seated height. Therefore, very often employees request that the desk be kept at a standard desk height, which reduces the need for an adjustable height desk.

Retrofit Sit/Stand Desks

If a company wants to offer the sit/stand desk option, retrofit sit/stand desks are devices that are placed on top of a standard desk or attached to a static desk to give the static desk some adjustability. I feel it is important to distinguish between these two types of retrofits: the type that sits on the desk and the type that attaches to the desk. There are quite a number of retrofit sit/stand desks on the market that can be used to raise the keyboard and/or the mouse and/or the monitor on the desk. I have found that the units that sit on top of the desk, without clamps or attachments to the desk, are very often actually a safety hazard. While monitors have gotten lighter over the years, they are still large heavy objects that can break and expose sharp edges. I have personally had monitors fall on me while attempting to adjust retrofit sit/stand components that do not have any type of clamps or fasteners. Therefore, I want to be sure to distinguish the different varieties of retrofits and divide them into categories that may make them easier to understand and evaluate prior to purchase.

Static retrofit sit or stand units that sit on top of a desk without any kind of clamps:

These are typically the least expensive of all of the units available. In fact, I have seen workstations where employees have actually created static retrofit sit/stand desks out of boxes, books, or bricks. The important feature these static retrofit sit/stand units must have is that all of the components of the workstation are at the appropriate heights. The employees also have to arrange a way of working while sitting down so as to alternate positions regularly and not stand too much. Static retrofit sit/stand units that are available pre-made are often plastic or even cardboard and, therefore, not reliably stable. With their dual drawbacks of encouraging prolonged static standing and their frequent flimsiness, I recommend caution when considering this type of unit.

Static standing retrofit units that clamp to the desk have the same negatives as static standing units that sit on top of a desk, but do not have the tipping safety risks of units that do not clamp onto the desk.

Adjustable retrofit sit/stand units that sit on top of the desk without any clamps:

These are typically the second least expensive of all units. Some brands on the market right now have become very popular, but I consider them actual safety hazards. ‡‡Adjustable retrofit sit/stand units that sit on top of the desk often adjust by using pneumatics with some type of squeeze handle as a release mechanism. The sections of the desk that lift and lower depend on the brand. Often, the user has to manually move the keyboard and mouse when alternating positions.

The monitor is usually placed on top of the unit, without a clamp, and cannot be adjusted in height independent of the desk. There is also a very small range available to adjust the monitor's distance from the user's eyes. The lack of monitor adjustability is one of the biggest negative aspects of these units. If the monitor is put on a monitor riser to correct the height, and then placed on top of the retrofit unit, the whole arrangement will be extremely unstable. Instead, the monitor has to remain at an incorrect height and the user simply accommodates to the height

---

‡‡- *While I realize many readers would like for me to say here which brands are good and which bad, that is not my place in this book. Rather, I want to give you a way of doing an objective evaluation prior to purchase or give you resources to call on to do the objective evaluation prior to purchase.*

as set. If you have an employee who has reported upper back, neck, or shoulder discomfort, this type of unit would not be a good solution. In fact, this unit could actually make that discomfort worse. I consider these units to have significant safety issues because of the instability of the monitor and because I have seen these units, lacking attachment points, slide off the desk.

Retrofit adjustable sit/stand units that clamp to the desk:

This type is slightly less expensive than replacing the whole desk, but has many of the advantages of a full desk replacement. The retrofit adjustable sit/stand units that clamp to the desk do not have the safety concerns associated with units that do not clamp to the desk. The monitor also typically clamps directly to the center of the sit/stand unit, allowing the user to adjust the height of the monitor based on need, but still have the monitor safely attached. The retrofit adjustable clamp-on units also have the ability to adjust between sitting and standing. But there is a caveat here —not all adjustable sit/stand retrofit units that clamp to a desk go low enough to be used without also raising the chair and using a foot rest. In other words, this retrofit gives employees a standing work area that is adjusted correctly, but does not necessarily provide employees a sitting work area that is adjusted correctly unless a footrest is added.

There are a number of retrofit adjustable clamp-on sit/stand units currently available on the market that have keyboard trays attached as part of the unit. The tray goes below the height of the desk just like a standard keyboard tray. With this configuration, the retrofit sit/stand clamp-on unit becomes a true sit/stand desk. When the user sits, he sits with his feet on the floor and the unit comes down to him. When the user stands, she can stand upright with the monitor, keyboard, and mouse at the correct heights.

Unfortunately, the majority of the units have monitor clamps that do not allow the depth of the monitor to be adjusted. An employee with reading lenses who uses this type of unit may have difficulty moving the monitor into a position where it is easily read. Conversely, someone who has good vision may feel that the monitors are too close for comfort; however, the monitor cannot be moved away. The employee also may have difficulty adjusting the monitor into the correct visual angle and distance if he uses progressive lenses. Employees who use reading or progressive lenses have to look through the bottom of their lenses with their head tilted up because the monitor is shifted slightly relative to their position.

Adjustable sit/stand desks

Moving away from the idea of a retrofit, we then come to the idea of replacing the desk completely from a static desk to an actual sit/stand desk. A true sit/stand desk has the capacity to go from the low-seated position to a high standing position easily and frequently throughout the day. The most common types of adjustable sit/stand desks use pneumatics or electric hoists to move the desk up and down. The more effort the user has to make to move the desk, the less often the user will switch from sitting to standing and back. Pneumatic desks need to be adjusted after installation based on the amount of weight that is on the desk. Once that is done, the desk should be very easy to move up and down. Typically, with the pneumatic sit/stand desk, a method of raising the monitor is still needed. A monitor arm is preferable to a monitor riser for the sake of better stability and safety.

The benefit to having an electric desk instead of a pneumatic desk comes when the control panel is upgraded to have programmable controls, for an additional cost, of course. With programmable controls, the ergonomics expert or paraprofessional can program in the correct heights for the employee for a variety of tasks throughout the day, usually three or four settings.

For example, the employee who does more paperwork than computer work can have the desk set for seated reading, standing reading, and standing computer work. Another employee, who works more on the computer than with paperwork, may have the desk set for seated computer, standing computer, and standing paperwork. When the desk does not have the ability to be programmed, employees often have to mark somewhere on the walls to show where the desk should be for various activities. As I mentioned earlier, many people do not have good internal awareness of the body's position in space. Teaching employees to use their bodies as reference markers correctly is very difficult. Many employees prefer a visual cue to know that they're putting their desks at the right height. If you don't mind marks on your walls, it is well worth it for the sake of advantages gained. If you're putting this much money into a desk system, it may be worth the extra hundred dollars or so to get the programmable type. Conversely, do not let the additional cost of the programmable mechanism stop you from considering replacing static sitting desks with sit/stand desks.

Chairs

I promised to take a moment to talk to about some chair adjustments that are available, so that you can have an intelligent conversation with either your interior designer or your ergonomics expert. I will start this section with the statement that there are hundreds, if not thousands, of chairs out there on the market and each one has a different way of marketing it features. There are too many variables for me to describe here, but I give you some of the basics:

Seat pan:

The seat pan is the part of the seat that you sit on. If the seat pan is adjustable in both length and width, the chair will fit the most users. Seat pan *length* is usually adjusted by something called a seat slider, a mechanism that literally slides the seat forward and backward.

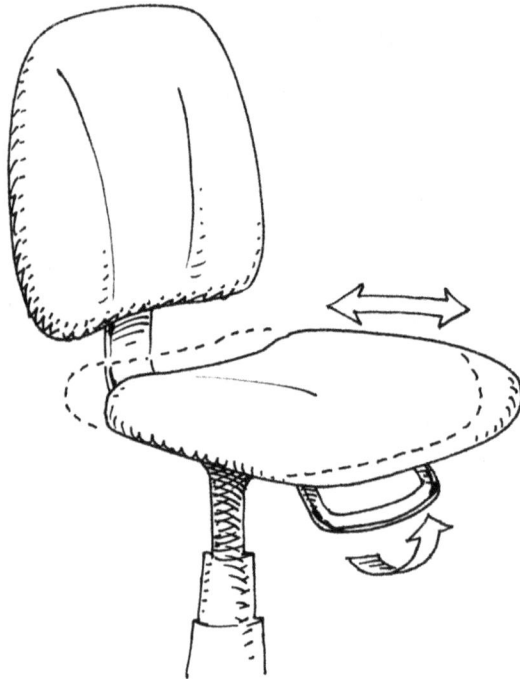

Figure V: Seat pan depth adjustment

Seat pan *width* is adjusted by the ability to move the armrests closer to the seat or farther away from the seat. At minimum, companies should have a chair with some adjustability so as to fit a good number of users. For companies that have a lot of employees, or have a heterogeneous employee population with a wide variety of cultures and genders, and therefore heights and weights, I recommend that they consider a chair brand with multiple styles that are adjustable and available in different sizes, e.g., big and tall or petite. The greatest difficulty that companies face is that they invest in chairs based on aesthetics, and then find that the chair style does not fit a wide range of employee body types. The company then has to purchase chairs to fit the large or small employees, and the new chairs don't look anything like the others in the office.

For example, if there is an employee who is very short, say, 5 feet tall, he may not fit within the range of adjustments on your standard chair. If you ensure that you have selected a chair that has sister chairs, so to speak, of the same style but different size, you can select a smaller chair for that one person, but maintain a consistent office appearance). One of the complaints I hear from HR and facilities managers is that, when an employee gets a bariatric chair or a super small petite chair that doesn't look anything like the other chairs in the office, other staff wonder why this person gets a "special" chair. Often the "special" chair in the office is thought to be a better chair and, therefore, everyone else feels left out. When the chairs match, there is less attention to the "special" chair.

Lumbar or back height adjustability:

The lumbar support of a chair is the bump on the back of the chair that is supposed to fit right in the lumbar portion of the spine. The lumbar portion of the spine is right above a person's belt, where the spine curves inwards. Adjustability of the position of the lumbar support of the chair can either be accomplished by moving the curve itself with an internal mechanism or by moving the backrest as a whole. I recommend choosing a chair that offers lumbar adjustability in some way.

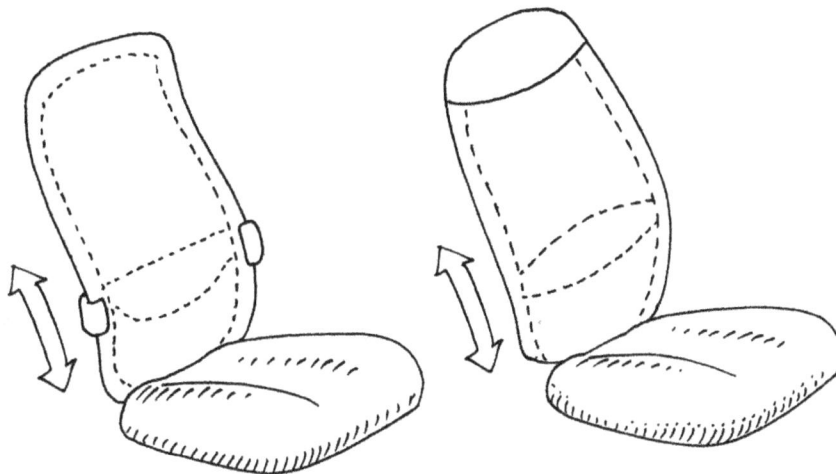

Figure W: Two methods of lumbar height adjustability

Some lumbar support mechanisms also allow for the depth, that is, the amount it pushes on the back, to be adjusted. The range of depth adjustments available within most mechanisms is actually very small unless the chair has an internal air bladder that can be filled to increase lumbar support. The majority of employees do not need adjustable lumbar depth unless the user has a pronounced lumbar curve.

Seat tilt:

Seat tilt is the ability for the seat pan to tilt backward on its axis so that the user's rear end drops lower than her knee, or forward so that the user's rear end is raised above knee height. The majority of users do not need this feature; however, if you have seat tilt, it helps when an employee needs extra encouragement to sit back in the chair. There are two main options for seat pan tilt: lock/unlock or infinite tilt-lock. Lock/unlock tilt chairs have certain angles at which the seat pan can be tilted and then locked into position. Many chairs simply lock in a flat position or are unlocked and bouncy. When chairs have an infinite seat tilt, the chair can be locked at any tilt angle within the range of the mechanism.

Seat recline:

Seat recline is not the same as seat tilt. Seat recline or backrest recline is the ability for the backrest to lean backwards. The backrest either moves independently of the seat pan itself so the chair can be made flatter like a first class airline seat, or in tandem with the seat pan, similar to a rocking chair. The majority of the large "executive" chairs are examples of chairs that do not have independent seat tilt and seat recline. Instead, the seat and the backrest are attached by the armrests and must move together.

Armrests:

Proper posture is when your arms are down by your sides with your elbows pointed toward your hips, or your arms hanging loose from your shoulders. Armrests should be able to be positioned just above the hip up against the waist. Armrests are not necessarily helpful for proper positioning (check back at fig P on page 75 for an illustration of armrests gone wrong). If the armrests are too deep, they hit the desk and push the user farther away from the desk or the keyboard tray. When the armrests hit the desk, the user ends up reaching for her keyboard, which causes her to slouch. However, when the armrests are in the proper position, directly under the person's shoulder, the armrests tend to catch on the person's hips every time they get in and out of the chair. If the armrests are not in the right position, the person is sitting like a chicken with her arms winged out to the side. This winged posture increases the tension at the neck and shoulders and increases the risk for neck and shoulder discomfort.

Headrests or neck rests:

Headrests and neck rests comprise two categories in ergonomics: a status symbol and a usable tool. The majority of users do not need headrests and neck rests. When a person sits in a chair that has a backrest that goes up higher than the person's shoulder or head, the person is perceived as being high up in the company structure. From a functionality standpoint, headrests and neck rests are actually fairly useless. In order to use a headrest or neck rest, the person has to lean backwards or push his head backwards. That means that he would need to stare up at the ceiling. In fact, headrests and neck rests, if placed in the proper position to be used while the person sits upright looking at the computer, often will cause the person to jut his head forward. The user is receiving tactile input on his hair or neck that something is back there, and he reflexively pulls away from the constant touch.

Lighting

One component of an office that we have not discussed yet is lighting. The lighting component of office design has generated quite an interesting discussion recently because of the move towards more natural lighting and open space designs. Believe it or not, some of the biggest recent complaints from employees have to do with migraines and other headaches because of the overabundance of light. There are two important features of lighting to take into consideration: the direction of the light and the purpose of the light.

General lighting or ambient lighting ensures that people do not run into or trip over things. This can come from direct overhead lights, such as can lights or fluorescent bulbs, or from more indirect sources. Direct light sources that are placed over the employee's head, or just in front of the employee's eyes, increase the strain on the eyes and contribute to complaints of headaches or glare. The best lighting for general light is what's called up-lighting or indirect lighting, as it does not irritate a person's eyes as much as direct lighting or spotlighting. Up-lighting or indirect lighting is a light source that first bounces off something else, such as the light fixture's reflector or a white wall, before reaching the eye.

If the purpose of the light is to illuminate detailed work such as paperwork, or to illuminate small tools such as those used by jewelry makers or for electronics wiring, then this requires more direct lighting. This direct light is called **task lighting**. Task light sources should be placed lower than the user's eye height so that it points directly onto the work and has limited direct illumination into the person's eyes. Task lighting is often achieved by what are called "task lamps." As we move towards increasing the natural light sources available from exterior windows, the need for overhead direct lighting sources is reduced.

All light sources need to be evaluated to determine whether the light bounces or glares off of the computer screen. The computer screen should be aligned at a 90-degree angle from any windows that receive direct sun. Employees should have control over the window coverings to ensure that light intensity and direction can be controlled on an as-needed basis. As we move towards "green" design, companies are computerizing window coverings, removing all control from the employees. The control computer is attempting to reduce the amount of electricity used by the electric lights. Therefore, as there is more natural light available, the computer will dim the interior lights and raise the shades. If the user has a monitor that is in direct line with the windows, she now has increased glare on the screen or increased light just behind the screen with no way to reduce that light. Consider the glare or overabundance of light when you are working with your interior designer on your green design.

Chapter 11: To Sit or Not to Sit?

Since the media has placed a lot of focus on the idea of sitting being bad for you, I want to spend a little extra time on the benefits and contraindications for sitting. Now that you understand the different types of furniture available, which one should you buy? Should there be a focus of exercising while working? Does it really come down to a type of furniture?

First, there is no rule that says that a person has to work sitting down. The tendency to work sitting down continues to be perpetuated because our computers are at the desk level. The majority of children are taught from a very young age that you sit to work. It is important to note that the idea that sitting all day, or being sedentary, is not good for general health and well-being is not a new concept. The promotion of movement throughout the day has been seen in the literature since the early 17th century.

Unfortunately, with the increased publicity of the concept of reducing the amount of time sitting throughout the whole day, the anti-sitting movement has narrowed the focus to your desk. In essence, the anti-sitting movement has blamed our poor behavior on an inanimate object. But is the blame targeted in the correct direction? If desks are changed to standing desks, wouldn't everyone get healthy? Standing desks have actually been in use for many years and we have not seen a corresponding improvement in the overall health of the workforce.

Research has shown that the lack of physical movement throughout the day is not solely based on furniture design. Instead, the lack of movement is a complex combination of:

- general behavior, e.g., seat seeking behavior at home and at work;

- the sedentary nature of the jobs being done at work, including computer work, paperwork, and meetings;

- the overall office furniture design, such as seated desks, seated meeting areas, seated breakrooms;

- the tools used to complete work, such as the computer versus portable paper;

- company policies and corporate cultures of sitting to work,

- and lack of reinforcement from management to increase movement throughout the day.

Critically important is a general lack of understanding that there is a big difference between *movement* and *standing* . [23] [24] [25]

Extended standing research has shown that there are health risks to prolonged standing; employees who do their jobs standing need opportunities to sit. Remember, there is a large working population that has been forced to stand in the past, from security guards to checkout clerks. Ergonomics principles have always recommended that employees be able to move throughout the day, alternating between seated work, standing work, and walking around work.

There is a lack of solid research available regarding how long someone should sit before it becomes "too long," or how long someone should stand before it becomes "too long," or how to get the benefit of both seated and standing working postures without exceeding the body's tolerances for either sitting or standing. Extended sitting creates higher back compression forces than does standing. Extended standing causes higher back compression forces than walking or standing with one foot propped up on a short step.[26] Standing, however, requires additional muscular forces in order to maintain posture compared to sitting. In my observations, most adults cannot tolerate static standing for more than 30 minutes before losing postural stability. Static standing, or standing without moving around, also puts a lot of pressure on the circulatory system of the body, and we see resulting lower leg swelling and joint pain. Poor posture is also prevalent in both sitting and standing as the body fatigues or becomes stiff.

Unfortunately, research is showing that approximately six months after being issued a new type of desk, such as a sit/stand desk, employees will stop using the sit/stand features correctly. The employees either stand for too long or have reverted back to a seated work posture. There is some discussion in the furniture development world about having desks that move on their own based on a schedule, but quite frankly, I'm a little concerned about furniture thinking for us.

> The best position is the next position.

The majority of employees who currently work at desks have jobs whose essential functions deal with knowledge—employees who need to produce reports, communicate via technology, and process information. The essential function is not to be attached to a computer for extended periods of time; using the computer for extended periods is actually just a tool to get the job done.

With this in mind:

Are sit/stand desks necessary to allow for movement throughout the day and, therefore, improved general health of your employees?

No.

However, sit/stand desks combined with reinforcement to change behaviors and culture can be very effective.

A few alternative methods to increase movement throughout the day:

- New work rule: when hands are not on the keyboard or mouse, the body does not need to be in the seat. Cell phone use, meetings, and paperwork can all be done standing.

- Switch one or two conference rooms into sit/stand areas where there is a mix of café tables and seated tables.

- Create phone rooms with counters instead of seats.

- Challenge managers to find enjoyable methods to break up workdays with movement time.

If you would like a good laugh, go look at The Onion's media blast about alternative working postures: http://www.theonion.com/video/more-office-workers-switching-to-fetal-position-de-36240. (Note: The Onion is a satirical news website and is not meant to be taken seriously.)

An additional low-cost option for increasing movement throughout the day is to institute a policy supporting walking meetings. Many companies that institute the walking meeting plan produce a lanyard for meeting participants to wear that requests that others please not disturb the meeting in progress. The company creates a culture that accepts that walking and talking in an area that will not disturb others is a positive occurrence. Walking meetings work well when there are 2 to 3 people maximum. Walking meetings work well during brainstorming sessions and often work to decrease the general tension of difficult meetings. Walking meetings do not work well when the topic under discussion is confidential, related to negative work performance, or a meeting that requires a lot of note-taking. However, I have seen people carry a cell phone with a recording program so notes can be dictated as needed. The use of a cell phone or recorder also provides an opportunity for the attendees to confirm that they were heard correctly because the note taker repeats what was said.

I was recently asked to design a conference room that was only for standing conferences. Unfortunately, a meeting room that requires the attendees to stand would conflict with basic principles of inclusion. We cannot assume that we know who in our group needs to sit down, and we cannot assume that everyone in attendance can stand up. Therefore, a compromise was made: a note on the wall in each of the conference rooms stating that attendees are encouraged to stand and move around during meetings. The note then went on to describe how to increase movement during the meeting in a respectful fashion such as not blocking other participants when standing.

Alternative Desks

Treadmill Desks

Treadmill desks take the concept of increasing movement throughout the day to a new level. Numerous variations of treadmills that go under a desk have now been developed and are available on the market. There are positives and negatives to using a treadmill desk. First, a treadmill in a workplace is a high liability for the company. If someone falls off or has a heart attack, it can be considered a workplace injury or death. Many companies I've seen have great difficulty with even including automatic defibrillators on their work floors in fear of them being misused, let alone putting a piece of exercise equipment in an office. There has been a lot of debate about whether the liability to the company can be mitigated with the use of proper forms, proper training, and safety lockouts on the unit. As of the publication of this book, I have not seen forms that are foolproof at reducing your liability. That being said, there are a number of companies that have implemented treadmill desks. The use is usually accompanied by stringent warnings, disclosures, and, of course, forms.

A treadmill at the workplace is supposed to be used for short periods of time spread throughout the day. There are very few people out there who can walk a marathon all day every single day. So when you are considering the implementation of a treadmill desk system, you have to take into account cost versus use. The most common solution I have seen is that companies will buy a few treadmill desks and put them in a shared workspace area. Employees sign up for short periods of time to come and work remotely on networked computers. Overall, I have not heard a lot of negatives about this type of arrangement, and it seems to be a good balance between encouraging movement and balancing budgets.

Another consideration is that desk treadmills are not designed to be used at a fast pace while working. The majority are actually locked so they cannot go above two or two-and-a-half miles per hour. For most people, that is a gentle stroll. Therefore, it needs to be understood that these workstations are not replacing a person's need to get a sufficient amount of exercise throughout the week. If the goal is to get your employees healthier, other methods will need to be in place to complement the reduction in time spent in seated work.

The primary drawback to treadmill desks is that the research that's currently available, the majority of which was done by companies who sell treadmill desks, has been done on very small numbers of people. What this means is that it is difficult to understand and generalize how a treadmill will affect the general workforce. There are two separate areas of research needed: evaluate how the use of a treadmill during work affects someone's health behaviors, and evaluate how walking on a treadmill affects their work productivity.

The research completed so far by impartial parties has shown two results of interest. First, a person's ability to accurately type and process complex information decreases treadmill workstation use. In other words, these small studies have shown that productivity can go down while someone works on a treadmill. The theory is that this decrease in productivity is because people cannot actually multitask well. The mental load required to maintain an upright position and keep pace while on a treadmill reduces the mental power available for the complex task of typing and processing information.

Second, a person's energy level, or feeling of alertness, has been shown to increase after a short time of treadmill use. In other words, productivity goes down while on the treadmill, but can potentially go up afterwards if a person is given time to walk on the treadmill. This result can actually be interpreted three different ways. Conclusion one: Treadmill desks are beneficial to the workplace because they increase productivity overall. Conclusion two: Activity increases productivity, and therefore employees should be encouraged to visit a gym in the middle of the day so that employees can exercise on a treadmill under gym supervision. Or, conclusion three: This research is a simple confirmation of known ideals—productivity increases if employees take more movement breaks. The research does not show that "up and moving" has to be on a treadmill, just that movement increases productivity.

Bicycle Desks

This brings me to another new piece of equipment to hit the market, a bicycle desk. A "bicycle desk" can be a desk attached to a stationary bike or simply a bike or elliptical without a seat or handles that slides under a desk. A bicycle desk has a number of severe limitations. When seated on a standard bike and riding through the countryside, your upper body is engaged in maintaining your balance and keeping you upright. You are secured only at your groin to allow your legs to move freely on the pedals. In order to make the seat more functional in an office environment, the bicycle desk is designed similarly to a recumbent bike system. The user sits in a chair and cycles with the legs. If you look at a traditional recumbent bike, you'll notice that the user is actually sitting low relative to the pedals and the user's knees often move above the hip line. In order to use the bicycle in a desk situation, the user has to slouch down in the seat to allow for freedom of movement in the hips. Also, recall that in order to promote proper posture, the keyboard and mouse must be directly above the user's lap. If the keyboard and mouse sits on a bicycle rider's lap, then the keyboard and mouse would move every time the legs cycle. The only way to reduce the movement of the keyboard and mouse would be to slouch down in the chair further.

Ball Chairs

There is absolutely no research supporting the use of therapy balls as chairs. Contrary to prevalent myths, the use of a balance ball as a method to increase exercise throughout the day and improve posture is completely false.

First, a person cannot exercise all day long--that is what would be required to balance on a ball all day. Employees who try to use a balance ball as an office chair are observed to hold a correct posture for short periods when simply balancing on the ball. Once the employee engages with the work activities, his posture degrades until it is worse than what would be seen if he were to sit badly in a good chair. The balls do not allow you to roll under the desk. Thus, in order to use the keyboard and mouse, the employee needs to reach forward, which results in poor posture.

Another consideration is that balance balls are a severe liability to your company. There have been numerous cases of fractured wrists and head injuries when either the employee who sits on the ball falls off or other people trip over the ball when it rolls into public spaces. I do not recommend balance balls be allowed in your office unless the employee is under very specific monitoring by a therapist. The supervising therapist must either see the workstation or work with your ergonomics expert to be sure that the employee can work safely and correctly.

Manufacturers have tried to make the balance ball safer for the workplace by supporting the ball with a frame. The end result looks something like a chair with the seat cut out and a ball stuffed in. I find it extremely interesting that the ball in a frame chair would even be considered a replacement. The whole point of sitting on a ball is having an unstable surface that you need to use your core muscles to balance. When you put the ball in a frame it is no longer an unstable surface. There is no research to say that a therapy ball or a ball in a frame achieves any positive goals. In addition, there is significant research that says balance balls are dangerous.

Chapter 12: Redefining the "Office"

Telework

In many workplaces, employees elect to work from home. In some cases, employees are required to work from home a certain number of days per week. Telework presents a very interesting ergonomic challenge. The courts and workers' compensation boards have not yet been confronted with enough complaints about telework related injuries for me to give you a conclusive answer about what is required of a company or what injuries a company may be responsible for if they occur in an employee's home.

If your ergonomics program includes individual evaluations, there may be a logistical nightmare and a high cost to evaluating teleworker spaces that are spread out over the state, country, or world. In response, many companies with ergonomics programs have put out guidelines requesting that employees who work from home take online assessments or use remote evaluation services. However, this raises the question as to how much equipment the company should pay for if needed.

If you have a flat amount available for at least partial purchase assistance, I find that many employees are willing to make an investment to benefit their own health. The monies directed towards ergonomics equipment for the home can be some of the smaller items, such as footrests and monitor risers, that solve many ergonomics problems. Overall, the best recommendation I can make is that the company provide as much education as possible and carefully consider the telework policy as it relates to work-related musculoskeletal disorders. As telework becomes more popular, I am sure that more regulations and, unfortunately, standards set by court cases, will follow.

Road Warriors

As businesses become more global, we are finding more employees on the road, in the air, and in coffee shops. It is perfectly normal in many areas of the country to conduct a majority of the workload outside of the office. Each remote location has ergonomics concerns.

Hotels

When employees work in multiple locations and have to travel for work, they often work in hotel rooms. There are many mobile devices involved in this scenario, and each one has positives and negatives. Hotel rooms, while they may have a desk and chair, were really not designed for intensive work. That does not mean that hotel spaces cannot be modified, but it does take some effort. On a recent trip, I was faced with a situation where I had to work on my laptop for extended periods, but the hotel's chair did not tilt back at all and the desk was very high. Instead of attempting to adjust the chair and the desk, I chose to use pillows to work up against the bed.

Figure X: Modified workstation in a hotel

As you can see, this solution allowed me to stay in an upright posture with my feet well supported and the laptop elevated slightly. It was not a perfect solution, but it was free and quick. Your employees who travel need to know these problem-solving techniques, such as using pillows, the trash can, the bed, or the chair in creative ways. Employees should be encouraged to consider what needs to be brought along on the trip to help make work more comfortable.

Coffee Shops and Restaurants

Coffee shops and restaurants are not wonderful places to work for extended periods of time from an ergonomics perspective. I recommend that an employee who works in this environment sit at a regular table, not in one of the comfy chairs, so that the laptop or other portable device can be supported on the table. Use of a laptop riser would elevate the screen and allow the person's head to come up over their shoulders while the keyboard moves closer to the body. If the person chooses to sit in one of the comfy chairs that the coffee shops give you to encourage you to drink more coffee, I would recommend that the portable device be put on top of a bag or briefcase to create a situation similar to what I did with pillows in the hotel.

Cell Phones

The cell phone is a device that we all appear to be attached to, whether we travel or not. However, it is important to know that cell phones were not designed to be a primary workspace. The act of typing on a phone keyboard puts your body into a very poor rounded posture. Cell phone work should be seen as a method of quick communication, unless dictation software is utilized. Fortunately, dictation software on phones has become better and is no longer quite so frustrating.

Cell phones also have increased employees' stress levels with the expectation of constant communication and availability. Believe it or not, employees can start to have an immediate stress response, such as elevated blood pressure, when exposed to a cell phone ring. This stress response is not even limited to the person whose phone has rung; people around them also show the stress response.

Employees (and teens) very rarely unplug. Employees often have one or two cell phones in constant communication with the office, home, relatives, colleagues on the road, and social media. Increasingly, companies are recognizing that being constantly hooked into electronic devices is unhealthy. In a world that is very high stress, companies are now discussing how to unplug their employees. The issue is that, when work is part of the global economy, very often employees are dealing with people in very different time zones.

The lack of ability to unplug is partially a cultural issue. There is a perception that any email that is sent should be responded to very quickly. Oftentimes, employees report that they feel that others will perceive a slight or insult if an email does not receive a quick reply. Interestingly, when asked, other employees will often say that the email was sent simply because they wanted to write it down before they forgot, not because a response was expected. The perception of immediate gratification increases the risk of RSI because it increases the likelihood that your employees will be working on devices that were never meant to be primary work tools. There is a mountain of research that connects stress with musculoskeletal aches and pains. Stress management often becomes part of a wellness or even ergonomics program because there is such a strong link between stress and musculoskeletal injury.

Figure Y: See the portable turtle within

Tablets

While tablets have gotten more popular, lighter, more powerful, and more adaptable, these devices are still not a replacement for a desktop in terms of ergonomic adjustability. Tablets, just like phones, require the user to lean down into that turtle position I mentioned in the chapter on the basic rules of ergonomics. If someone is going to travel with a tablet, I recommend traveling with an external keyboard. There are many very light external travel keyboards available on the market. The external keyboard allows the tablet to be raised closer to eye height while the keyboard stays low. If a tablet will need to be used in a car (while parked, of course), there are a few devices that attach to the steering wheel to hold the tablet up higher. Again, the point is to raise the person's head and bring the keypad closer so that the user bends at the elbows instead of reaching forward.

Air Travel

Airplane travel has one additional component not seen in other forms of travel—being stuck in an airline seat. I have had several companies ask me what their travel upgrade policy should be from an ergonomics perspective. Is there really a correlation between the airline seats and back problems? The answer: somewhat yes and somewhat no. The seats are not very good at all, true. However, the issue with air travel is usually not the seat, unless you are a lot wider or longer than the seat itself, but the amount of time spent seated. A travel upgrade usually puts someone in business class or higher, which opens up the personal space allotted. The increased space, in essence, gives flyers more cultural permission to stand. This really isn't a function of the class of travel, but in the perception of freedom.

From a recommendation standpoint, all I can tell you is that the seats in all classes of airlines are not adjustable, are not supportive, and are not designed to be sat in for long periods of time. Instead of an upgrade, I often recommend that people choose aisle seats so that they feel that it is acceptable to stand up every hour and stretch. On overseas flights, the flyer can lie down if in a business class or first class seat. From an ergonomics perspective, it is better to sleep flat than sleep with your head on the tray or on your shoulder.

Luggage

Managing luggage is also a very important part of travel. There is a trend now to refuse to check any luggage in order to reduce the time spent waiting for luggage to arrive on the carousel in baggage claim. This means that travelers pack very large, heavy carry-on bags and have to lift them up into the overhead bins. Needless to say, it is not recommended that employees haul and lift if not taught to do so properly. It is recommended that employees be encouraged to check luggage as a means of reducing injury. However, I also recommend that your employees be trained on how to safely retrieve luggage from the carousel. You can find more about material handling strategies in the industrial portion of this book that follows. I consider luggage handling in the same category as industrial lifting.

Conclusion: The Benefits of a Good Ergonomics Program in the Office Setting

When it comes to office ergonomics, I truly believe that it is in the best interest of a company to do more than just check the box with a lunch and learn or a health fair. As we've discussed, the number of people who have reported problems does not equal the number of people who have problems. At minimum, have a method to provide assistance in response to employee complaints of pain to address employee concerns before the employee needs to go to a doctor.

To review, what does an ergonomics program look like?

A "check the box" program:

Provides some group education in the form of lunch and learns or health fairs. Overall, this will not create much change, but at the same time does not require a significant budget.

A good program:

Provides individual assessments as needed to address the needs of employees who have reported aches and pains. Overall, this will be an expensive solution and runs the risk of more and more people deciding to come forward with complaints. However, it is a positive measure as you will start to hear about the problems and, therefore, be able to get a sense of the magnitude of the situation.

A very good program:

Provides individual assessments to people who report aches and pains and provides regular walk-through fast assessments for anyone who puts in a request. Overall, a moderately expensive solution that is moving in the right direction. Again, this is a positive measure to start to get an idea of the scope of the situation.

An excellent program:

- Provides individual assessments to people who are "in pain."

- Provides education and walk-throughs on a regular basis to people who want help.

- Provides training on how to set up the workstation during the on-boarding process.

- Has a reminder program to reinforce change.

- Encourages movement and participation in an active work behavior.

This program will be expensive at first, but has the greatest impact for the longest period, with decreasing costs corresponding to increasing reach.

The next section of this book will be focused on industrial settings. However, I recommend that even HR professionals who do not have employees who work in industrial settings skim through the next section because all employees at some time or another will lift a case of paper and participate in home activities that have associated risks. The ultimate step for an office ergonomics program is to be able to move beyond teaching employees just about desk ergonomics and start teaching employees about how to protect their bodies from injuries with everyday activities.

Part 4: How to Set up Ergonomics Programs in an Industrial Setting

What is Meant by an "Industrial Setting" in This Book?

For our purposes, industrial settings include any situations of manual material handling or physical labor. This can include everything from yard work to labor in manufacturing plants. Each company has its own unique situation, so this section will focus on broad ergonomics concepts and programming needs for workers who do not sit at desks for most of their workdays. Some companies have employees who do the same things every day, and some have employees who confront a variety of tasks and problems every day in varying environments. My favorite groups to work with are utility and service crews who go out into the wild world (also known as "the field") to work in different locations, often in extreme environments, and then come back the next day and work in a new location. The challenge faced by employees who work out in the field, and not in a structured manufacturing plant, is that engineering controls are not always available.

This section includes how to set up a successful program as well as examples of the measurements used by the ergonomics experts to determine risk. I believe that having a basic understanding of how ergonomics professionals evaluate job tasks gives you the background knowledge necessary to have intelligent conversations regarding programs and solutions. In the Appendix, I will provide you with a list of industrial measurements used by ergonomics experts along with a basic explanation of the equations involved. The measurements and equations are explained not because I expect you to go out and measure for yourself, but because I think is important for you to understand the results and conclusions presented by your expert.

Chapter 13: Program Components

The goal of all ergonomics programs is to reduce risk in an efficient and effective manner. Industrial ergonomics programs should be designed with this in mind; however, budget limitations do create some hurdles. There are many options for starting an ergonomics program, and multiple components for that program that should be considered, each with its own benefits and drawbacks.

Ergonomics programs in industrial environments do not necessarily deviate from the model used in office environments: evaluate and measure, report, and then control the risks. However, compared with office ergonomics, industrial tasks often require more intense focus on the evaluation and measurement phase before giving consideration to control measures. Industrial ergonomics programs, like office programs, still prioritize the tasks or jobs that present immediate risks before continuing to a more preventative model. Unlike office ergonomics programs, which are more tailored to individuals, ergonomics concerns in the industrial environment tend to focus on protecting the masses using standardized measures and normative data.

A review of the components of an ergonomics program:

- Evaluation and measurement

- Reporting

- Address the concerns through:

    1. Engineering controls

    2. Administrative controls

    3. Behavioral and individual controls

- Reinforcement

Evaluate, Measure, and Report

Programs that demonstrate the most effective interventions start in the evaluation phase. Unless you have already identified a job or task that has a significant number of injuries or can easily be designated as having high risk, the role of the first evaluation phase is to identify priorities. This prioritization can take a number of possible forms. For example, a broad ergonomics sweep or observation period for all major job titles by an ergonomics expert can help narrow down priority tasks that visually demonstrate risk. For example, employees are observed lifting objects poorly or frequently, physical movements are done repeatedly using small muscle groups, or environments are observed that may increase risk. In addition, the ergonomics expert can work with you to do the deep dive into your healthcare data or injury reporting data to identify common musculoskeletal injuries or trends in injuries. Priorities can be established by conducting interviews with experienced employees to determine risk areas that they have identified, but may not have reported.

Once several job titles or job tasks, i.e., smaller components of the job title, have been identified as priorities, only then does the in-depth evaluation of each task begin. It is important to understand that each small component of a job task should be evaluated both separately and as part of an extended chain of events. For example, if the job title identified as a priority is that of a plumber, then the tasks evaluated will be broken into such smaller components as: unloading the truck, installing a toilet, repairing a sink, and driving. It is not necessarily the job of *plumber* that is considered the risk. It is the essential functions of that job that are evaluated for risk.

An ergonomics assessment is an in-depth measurement of risk factors including weight, vibration, timing, repetition, and distances traveled. The ergonomics expert will bring tools that take objective measurements of the forces involved with the task. These measures are then plugged into calculations or compared to normative data. For example, ergonomics evaluations often include video footage of a job being performed. The video allows the evaluator to time repetitions, observe movement trends, and slow down action to note details not easily observable during the actual performance of a job. Ergonomics evaluations also include measurements of weights and distances traveled with basic scales and tape measures. Some of the more specialized equipment used includes a tool called a *push-pull dynamometer* that measures, as the name implies, how much force is needed to push or pull an object. For example, it would be used to measure the force needed to push a cart into movement from a stopped position or the pull force needed to maintain steady movement on a pulley.

The ergonomics report should include notations about the measurements taken and methods used to collect data. The methods description should provide an explanation about how the expert came to the proposed recommendations. The expert should be able to demonstrate the risk levels observed during the initial evaluation and what risk levels are expected after changes are made based on the expert's recommendations, if available. Some jobs or tasks are so complex that the current available measurement methods have to be combined to determine risk or smaller components of the job isolated for measurement with a specific tool. If we consider our plumber example, the analysis may first measure the forces involved with unloading tools necessary for a job, then the risks involved in carrying the tools to the job, then the ten different components of the job itself. In order to analyze the risks, the ergonomics expert may use five different measurement methods. The expert should be clear about the rationale for the conclusions made and any limitations of the calculations.

Before continuing on to methods for mitigating risk factors, I must take a moment to re-emphasize the importance of including the employees who are actually involved in the jobs in the evaluation and mitigation process. Again, employee participation not only improves acceptance of the ergonomics program; it also provides insider knowledge that an ergonomics expert does not have. The ergonomics person is not an expert in the functions of any particular job. Rather, she is an expert in teaching problem-solving using ergonomics principles.

Methods to Address the Risk Factors

Engineering Controls

Engineering controls focus on the reduction or elimination of risk factors through a change in the job tools, tasks, or environment. It is important to note that risks can be reduced by either decreasing the risk—for example lowering the weight of an object—or increasing the risk beyond human capability—for example increasing the weight of an object 10- or 100-fold and moving the task to a machine. The choice of direction to actually implement depends greatly on the situation and available resources.

To refresh your memory briefly from the "Rules of Ergo" section, some of the goals of engineering controls are to:

- Ensure that the loads and forces exerted by the employee do not exceed tolerances

- Ensure that the number of repeated movements do not exceed tolerances

- Keep the load sufficiently close to the worker's body to reduce reaching and improve the person's ability to use proper postural control

- Reduce the likelihood that the worker will twist the spine during the movement or load application

- Reduce the amount of time or distance over which the load must be managed

- Mitigate any negative environmental factors that may decrease the worker's tolerances

- Reduce any external pressures, vibrations, or contact points on the body

With engineering controls, it is common to consider a range of options and implement a combination of options to address each component risk area. I am simplifying the process and the issues here merely for the sake of demonstrating the process. The company may choose to address the highest measurable risk area only or even address the area of risk that is easiest to fix. There are a number of additional factors such as union acceptance, overall corporate plans and goals, and manufacturing limitations to consider. Sometimes, getting the fastest fix or addressing the item highest on the workers' list is the best way to give energy to the program.

Consider the challenges faced by ABC Widgets Company:

ABC Widgets has increased production of widgets recently and has added more staff to handle the increased load. ABC Widgets has a safety manager who is responsible for the OSHA logs. Shipping Department Manager Asher has had to shuffle some people around to handle all of the boxes being moved through his shipping department, and space is at a premium. Asher has noticed that shipping department staff are giving him ugly looks lately, and they stop talking when he comes over. He often complains to his supervisor, Tory, that his workers are constantly trying to get out of working. Asher complains to Tory that his staff doesn't listen to him. Tory has noticed that Asher's workers have increased their visits to the occupational nurse, and the shipping department has had two workers' compensation claims filed in the past six months, one for a back strain and one for a shoulder strain. She is concerned because that department did not have a workers' compensation claim in the preceding six months. An ergonomics sweep for engineering issues shows high risks for lifting the boxes from the delivery belt, the distance the boxes are carried, and the method of placing the boxes on a pallet.

At this point, what are Tory and Asher's options to reduce injuries?

We have a few engineering considerations:

The boxes themselves are selected as the focus of the initial ergonomics evaluation and, after measurement, the ergonomics expert recommends that the boxes be reduced in size to reduce each box's overall weight. That would mean that each worker would be moving more boxes, but each box would weigh less. From a business perspective, that may increase material costs or disrupt end users. Alternatively, the expert could recommend that the box size be tripled or quadrupled so that there would be justification for the installation of a machine that moves the boxes, thus eliminating the workers' handling of the boxes completely. From a business perspective, this would also impact materials cost and may also disrupt end users. It also may disrupt a process somewhere up the line—can the machines and belts working farther up the line even handle a box that big?

Conversely, if the initial evaluation focuses on the movement of the boxes onto pallets, the ergonomics expert may recommend that the pallets be placed on a rotating scissor lift inset in the floor. The pallet table rotates to keep the delivery area directly in front of the worker. The pallet table rotation reduces the need to step around or reach over the boxes that are already there. The scissor lift portion of the table keeps the delivery surface level directly in a worker's power zone. When the box is in the worker's power zone, the worker can use proper posture and engage the body's strongest muscles.

To reduce the distance traveled from the delivery belt to the pallets, the ergonomics expert could recommend that the pallets are stacked closer to the belt that delivers the boxes. In fact, if the budget is available, the expert could recommend that the end point (the pallet) be moved to the end of the mechanized belt so that the belt delivers the box directly onto the pallet.

Most likely, a combination of evaluations and recommendations would be made concurrently to account for the full chain of events. I have simplified it here to break down the thought process.

The importance of engineering controls is to remove or reduce the issues noted. However, it is important to note that administrative controls may need to be combined with engineering controls. For example, the shipping department may be very cold in the winter with the bay doors open all the time. Even after the material handling changes have been made, in the winter, management may need to implement a job rotation schedule so that no one is working in the cold environment for too long.

Administrative Controls

Administrative controls in the industrial setting are similar to those in the office setting. Administrative controls in the industrial setting may include job rotation or job sharing. A change in break schedules also would fall under this category. In a broad sense, any changes that are put into policies and procedures or standard operating procedure manuals become administrative controls.

Often, administrative controls are part of engineering controls. For example, in the case of ABC Widgets, use of the scissor lift may require a change in corporate policies to include mandatory training on how to use it safely. The addition of a new tool may require penalties to be documented for workers not using the tool in a safe manner. In this type of situation, administrative controls are used to reinforce the use of engineering controls.

Behavioral and Individual Controls:

Within the industrial setting, behavioral and individual controls typically take on two primary roles: increasing the workers' capability to tolerate the required forces and ensuring that workers have the knowledge to implement changes and protect themselves. Except in jobs such as emergency response, military, and some specialized jobs, physical fitness activities are typically considered as wellness or health behaviors. Many companies provide physical fitness facilities or facility discounts to increase employees' utilization of strengthening equipment, but physical fitness is not tested on a regular basis to determine whether employees have the strength, flexibility, or postural control necessary to perform the job tasks. It is more common for individual tolerance controls to take the form of personal protective equipment modified for an individual's needs, such as prescription protective glasses or gloves of various sizes.

On the other hand, it is extremely common and necessary for ergonomics programs to include some form of training to improve employee knowledge of safety and proper use of equipment. Ergonomics factors must be included in these training programs. Every time an engineering or administrative control is implemented, training is needed to help integrate the change into the workers' consciousness. The worst outcome for your ergonomics program would be to spend money on a new piece of equipment or to change a process, only to have no one use it; employees implement the control incorrectly and get hurt; or the new equipment or tool get damaged through incorrect use. I have even seen situations where training was not completed and the employees selected to re-modify the new equipment on their own to make it function more like the original tool. I cannot tell you the number of closets and storerooms I have opened to find brand new equipment sitting inside, dusty with disuse. That equipment would have addressed the risks identified in my assessment, but employees would not utilize the tools. The fault was not in the equipment itself but in the implementation of the control.

Training or behavioral changes are not limited to teaching someone to lift properly or use a tool properly. Training and behavioral control needs to create a conduit for cultural acceptance and participation within your workforce. As I travel around the world working in the field, I have found many instances where I needed to step back and rethink one of my recommendations because of how the working culture of that country, city, population, and workforce view and interact with their jobs and management. Company and national cultures change how trainings are conducted and must influence how we approach engineering or administrative changes.

It is important to separate the portion of the task that is under the employee's control from the part that is controlled by the employer. Employers control the tools used, portions of the environment where the work is completed, the supervision given, and the type of work done. Employees have varying levels of control of some of these items, but primarily have control over how they work.

Why do training classes often fail to have long-lasting results? There is actually a very simple reason: Adults cannot learn new movement patterns by just watching someone else do them. If I were going to try to teach you to play a sport or a musical instrument well enough to be paid to play, I could not just pop a video into a player or send you to a seminar. Imagine trying to learn to be a soccer star by watching videos and never kicking a ball. True, adults can learn from videos—I taught myself to crochet that way. However, in order to actually learn to do the movement well, adults have to practice the movement. Compared with children, adults have an additional problem with learning new movement patterns. Adults have previously-engrained movement patterns and a perception of how well they can perform those movements.

An additional factor affecting program success is that the participants must have some respect for the trainer or evaluator. That respect often is gained by having evaluations and trainings truly focused on what your employees do every day, not on generalities. Remember my favorite safety training story from the introduction? No one would have taken me seriously if I were the one teaching people how to use a chainsaw; I had never even held one before that day! You get better buy-in when programs are designed around the employees you are trying to influence, not by trying to make your employees re-design themselves around your training.

Obviously, I have not handled every tool out there, and I have definitely not done every job out there. So how do I garner respect? When I teach ergonomics to employees, the training is focused on how well they know their job. I am there to be taught the job and to work together with them to find solutions. I am not there as the expert. Instead, I am there as a team member. It is amazing how powerful the term team member is in these programs. If your employees are not a part of a team, what are they a part of? Define that and help the ergonomics expert utilize that in the ergonomics program.

Personally, when teaching ergonomic principles, I do not get into theory or engineering controls. Instead, I break it down into four rules that the employee can implement. In other words, you will notice that the rules do not say, "Make the tool lighter" or "Get out of the rain." The rules provide a problem-solving pathway. It asks the employee: Can you follow one or more of these rules to help protect yourself?

Here are my rules for employees:

Think first. I'm amazed by the number of times I have heard someone telling me about their injury and the explanation starts with "I just didn't think…" Well, there is your first problem. This moment of thought is there to give the worker time to make an assessment of what may or may not be under their control. This is also the time to encourage employees to analyze where engineering or administrative controls could be useful. Some of the best engineering controls I have seen have come from employee ideas and suggestions.

Close. Bring the object or tool closer to the body before engaging. This decreases the forces on the body. For example, if you pull your keyboard close to you, so that you are typing with your arms down by your sides, you decrease the pull on your neck and shoulders and increase the likelihood of sitting up. If you pull a 50-pound sandbag closer to you instead of picking it up straight off the center of a pallet, you decrease the spinal compression forces.

Square. At no point should the employee be twisting while working. For example, if your monitor is in one corner of your desk and you are spending your workday looking to the side, you are not doing yourself any favors. Going back to that 50-pound sandbag, workers often will twist their spines when swinging their upper bodies to pass the bag from one spot to another. Twisting is devastatingly bad for backs.

Big. This is my only rule that comes close to that old "lift with your legs" rule. I want your employees to be thinking about using a larger muscle or joint at all times, not just when lifting. For example, when pushing a lawn mower, you could turn the unit by just moving your arms. Instead, I want you to walk in an arch around the axis of the lawn mower so that you are using your body weight at all times. Keep the lawn mower in front of you and walk around it instead of pushing harder with one hand to twist and turn the mower.

I am not by any means discounting the need to measure and modify loads that are above safe lifting levels, move levers that are out of reach zones, or make other engineering changes. In fact,, if we consider ergonomics as a two-part process—fixing the problem and teaching people how to be part of the solution—then using these rules is a good way to approach teaching the employee problem-solving skills.

As mentioned previously, methods of providing training come in a variety of forms, from videos shown in a classroom to live classroom training to guided practice sessions. Since each company has its own budgetary constraints, I am providing some of the options here, with cost-to benefit-considerations.

Off-the-Shelf Training Programs

The lowest-cost component would be considered a back class or lifting class. These can be pre-packaged as non-customized live workshops where the instructor has never been on your site or seen what you do before, but comes to your site for training or with non-customized videos, thereby reducing the cost, compared with a live a trainer. Traditionally, back classes focus on how to lift basic objects such as bags and boxes. Off-the-shelf trainings usually consist of education like this: Here is a box, here is how you lift the box, and we want you to always lift in this way. These videos are generic so as to increase the customer base for the sake of sales. The generic training often shows people lifting in a controlled environment and focuses on the position of the spine and feet. In fact, this is where you will hear that age-old myth repeated, "Lift with your legs, not your back, and you will be safe."

As mentioned previously, evidence does not demonstrate that these pre-packaged workshops or videos are effective in either the short or long term. In industrial settings, generic workshops are even less effective than in the office setting because of the complexity of muscle patterns your employees are required to use on a daily basis, but generic workshops and videos are often implemented first because of their low cost.

Customized Programs: Classroom Only

Customized programs are more expensive because they require that a trainer be on site and use tools and equipment from your worksite as part of the workshop. Customization can include using actual job tools during the workshop, or using videos and pictures of the job that you have supplied. Customized classroom-only workshops are often less expensive than the classroom-plus-practice workshops described next because the workshop itself takes less time.

At least when programs are somewhat customized—for example when the trainer uses the actual item that the person will be lifting—employees have somewhat of a greater likelihood to implement at least a small amount of change following the workshop. There is some research to support the effectiveness of customized classroom-only workshops for accomplishing positive change, at least to a limited extent. Concepts and rules presented during the workshop can be memorized and repeated, but employees demonstrate difficulty with internalization of new movement patterns when they do not actually experience them first-hand.

> Consider what it would take to teach you how to be a professional soccer star. I show you a video of somebody kicking a ball. Could you go out and kick a ball correctly enough to even begin the process of becoming a superstar? If only it were that easy. Yet, for some reason, we assume that we can teach people who have already spent a long time doing their job a different way of doing it by showing them a video or by having them take a quick class on lifting a box.
>
> The most interesting work I do is when I teach workers how to shovel correctly. Employees who shovel dirt or shovel snow have a high rate of injury because of the high forces and repetitions of the job. Think about when you learned to use a shovel for the first time. For many of us who live in states where snow is abundant or gardening is available, we learn to use a shovel as very small children. It is unlikely that you learned how to use a shovel correctly when you were a child, at least from an ergonomics perspective.

Let's say that I put you in a classroom and tell you that I want you to forget everything you learned about shoveling. You will watch this video and learn how to shovel correctly.

The challenge is that you not only have to learn a new movement pattern, you have to delete an ingrained movement pattern. It is even harder to delete an old movement pattern than it is to learn a new one.

Customized Programs: Classroom Plus Practice

These are workshops that begin in a classroom or group lecture setting and are quickly followed by practice time both in a controlled setting and then in the normal work setting. For example, in the classroom setting, the employee may be told, "First, work with this tool here on stable ground;" then, in the normal work setting, he will be told, "Now, work with the tool in the hole you normally find yourself in." The classroom-plus-practice workshops are more expensive as they can often take two to three hours. However, they are more effective in the long run because of that added practice time.

Adults learn new movement patterns through repetition and generalization in multiple environments. They have to practice the new movement pattern not only in an artificially safe environment, but also in the actual work environment. If the employees have to work in multiple environments, then they have to be given the opportunity to practice the new patterns in a variety of situations.

Generalization, the ability to take information learned in one situation and apply it to another situation, is actually a learned skill. Movement patterns are even harder for people to generalize than simple information. For example, you learn that water is wet. You have learned the skill of generalization; therefore, you are able to understand that seawater is wet and water that comes out of the tap is wet. The concept that water is wet is knowledge that you need to use in multiple situations.

When an adult learns a new movement pattern, such as playing a new instrument, the brain creates new pathways to record this new pattern of movement—think of it as the body creating a new file folder under the heading of "movements." When an adult is asked to change an old movement pattern, the brain already has a file saved that it has accessed repeatedly, which makes it readily available in the brain's shortcuts menu. When asked to generalize a new movement, the brain will default to the original pattern. Even adults need time to understand that the same rules apply when a box is lifted inside a truck as it is outside the truck. On paper, this seems extremely simple, but in real life it is extremely complex. When a workshop includes time for practice, the brain is given the opportunity to create the movement pattern file and make it easy to access via the shortcut menu.

Reminder Programs

As with everything in life, change does not come easily. Therefore, it is important that all engineering, administrative, and behavioral controls be reinforced regularly. The least expensive and least effective method is through posters. After a while, posters become part of the background noise of our lives. Reminder programs are most effective when they are multifaceted: A combination of posters, verbal and written reinforcement, management effectiveness checks, worker engagement in continued improvement projects, and electronic reminders works best to remind your employees of the concepts taught. Reminder programs can also include a variety of reinforcements, such as rewards or punishments, to encourage certain behaviors.

Should ergonomics programs include rewards or punishments as part of the reminder process?

Brief reminder:

Positive = giving something to the person or group

Negative = taking something away from the person or group

Reward = action done to increase behaviors wanted

Punishment = action done to decrease behaviors not wanted

Examples we are all familiar with:

Positive reward: bonus pay for increased productivity

Negative reward: your boss stops visiting your office every day when you get the project done

Positive punishment: giving out demerits or detention for acting out

Negative punishment: docking pay for work not done

In general, while punishments have their place, they have not been shown to affect long- lasting positive change in the fluid culture of the workplace. It is somewhat easier to get an employee to do something you want them to do than it is to stop an employee from doing something they want to do.

I recommend that you include a method of measuring program effectiveness for all ergonomics programs. The act of measuring program effectiveness is also a prime opportunity to reinforce changes. As part of my own effectiveness check, I often ask the crews I have trained how much they remember from a previous class or discussion. If the crews remember the concepts, great, the training effected a change in the worker's memory. If the crews don't know the concepts covered in the training, fine, I have an opening to remind them of the concepts covered. Another way of using program measurement to reinforce change is to ask for feedback about an engineering control a few weeks or months after the control has been implemented. Such feedback questions can include: How many times do you use XYZ change? How many times do you find you can't use XYZ change? What supports you in the use of XYZ change? What prohibits you from regularly using XYZ change? If the workers look at you blankly, then you know you have a problem with the engineering control's integration into the job task.

When you engage your workforce to continue the process of improvement, you not only reinforce the changes made but are also opening channels for moving your program from reactive to proactive. The more workers are able to identify potential problems before they happen, the more you know they have integrated the "rules" of ergonomics and will work to keep themselves safe.

Reminders may seem simple, but as we mentioned with the poster idea, they can be difficult to make effective. In the industrial world, I prefer onsite reminders. Ergonomics leads, champions, or consultants spend time on the floor or out in the field talking to workers and actively reminding workers of processes and changes. Onsite reminders are especially important with jobs that do not have a set location and pattern, such as utility work or construction. Workers who have jobs that change every day need help onsite to learn how to apply the concepts to real-life situations.

Chapter 14: Applying Ergonomics Principles to Industrial Work

Now that we've talked about the development of an ergonomics program, the rest of this chapter is dedicated to how ergonomics concepts get applied to the movements and forces that industrial workers undergo on a daily basis.

Pushing and Pulling

Workers push and pull wrenches, dollies, carts, baskets, rolling shelves, heavy machinery, wheelchairs, gurneys, and objects hanging from the ceiling. While it is out of the scope of this book to detail the exact physics of all of these actions, some basic ergonomics strategies can be applied. The amount and direction of force necessary to start the movement, continue the movement, and stop the movement are all important to measure when evaluating push and pull forces and tasks. It is necessary to understand the forces required to overcome friction between the object and the floor even if the tools have wheels.[27] If working with a tool hanging from the ceiling, the forces applied must overcome the friction between the rollers and the track to get the object moving and continuing along its path. Then inertia must be overcome to safely stop the object and keep it from swinging if necessary.

Figure Z: Pushing with your back to the object

Pushing with your body against an object, such as when you turn around and use your back to move a bookcase or heavy cart, is the best way of distributing forces (see fig Z). Most times, your employees cannot turn around and put their backs to whatever object is being pushed. When exerting force on a cart, your employees may find it easier to pull while walking backwards because they can lean backwards and use body weight to move the cart. Pulling requires less muscular contraction of the arms, whereas pushing requires the person to engage their arm muscles to keep from falling into the object being pushed (see fig AA). It also must be mentioned that, while pulling backwards is easier for the body, it is also extremely unsafe as you cannot see where you are going or what you are stepping on. Just as with lifting, the body should never be twisted while pushing or pulling. The same ergonomics principles apply at all times-- items should be kept close and square, and manipulated with the largest muscle possible. The additional factor to consider with pushing and pulling forces is always to be cognizant of balance and the direction the employee may fall if either the tool or the employee should slip.

Figure AA: Pushing forwards

Lifting and Lowering

As mentioned in the "Rules of Ergo" section, in general we try to keep any objects that a person is lifting or lowering at a weight below 51 pounds. You will recall, too, that the 51-pound limit will decrease depending on the location of the object and how the object will be moved. As the object moves away from the body's central line and/or the distance of travel increases, the amount of pressure the back can support decreases.

Oftentimes, companies will recommend that employees team lift or group lift heavy objects that exceed the 51-pound limit. Team lifting, while it seems like a method to share the load, is not that effective in real-world applications. Conceptually, if you have a 90-pound object with two people lifting, each will get 45 pounds. However, the division of weight is not what actually happens. Perhaps if both employees were to stand on a perfectly level surface, while holding a perfectly level and evenly weight-distributed object, each employee may be lifting around 45 pounds. The issue is that very often the object is an awkward shape, has an awkward weight distribution, or cannot be lifted and lowered strictly up and down. Your employees carry, move, lift, and lower this object in some way. The acts of moving and carrying shift the object depending on the angles involved. As one employee steps up over a curb, for example, the employee on the other side of the object is pulled along and the object's weight shifts.

An easy way to conceptualize the uneven distribution of weight with team lifting is to consider what happens when friends get together to move a sofa upstairs. Which position would you want to be in—the person at the bottom of the stairs or the person at the top of the stairs? While this is a team lift, it is easy to see how it is not an equal lift. The person at the bottom of the stairs ends up with an unequal and very heavy load.

If there is an object that exceeds the recommended weight limits, the best situation would be to have a machine handle the object (an engineering solution). In situations where there is no machine available, then a team lift would be preferable to an individual lift—with caution. In the case where an object will be maneuvered on variable terrain, it is sometimes safer for one person to lift the object because there will be no sudden changes in weight or in position of the weight as the object is moved. The highest musculoskeletal risk occurs when the weight of an object being carried shifts suddenly and the body must accommodate the weight's movement. The body must compensate for a very sudden, very forceful, and possibly awkward position, which can very easily lead to an injury.

There are visible "warning signs" that can signal to even a layperson that the lift may be going wrong or an object is too heavy. When a person tries to exceed the body's tolerances for lifting, the person lifting often will push the object with his knee to get the object to waist height (see fig BB). People also start kicking the object or lifting it in a jerky fashion if the object is too heavy or the person is getting tired. Managers and staff should be taught this visual sign because it's fairly easy to see and identify as a cue to offer assistance to the person lifting. The visual sign also can be used as a trigger to activate an in-depth ergonomics assessment of the task.

Figure BB: Using the knee to push the object into a better grip

Carrying

The rules for carrying objects are the same as for lifting/lowering: The object should be kept close to the body with a good grip. Carrying, in the ergonomics world, is when we transport an object without changing the height of the object. That is, carrying can be completed without lifting or lowering. For example, when you pick up a box from one table and move it to another, there is no change in the height of the box. People often will carry more weight than they can lift because carrying allows the person to lock her arms and use locking of the joints to carry versus actually requiring muscular strength to bend her arms.

The visible warning sign that someone is carrying an object that is too heavy is a postural lean to the side or towards the back (see fig CC). This is observed often with parents when they hold children on one hip. The parent looks like she is trying to counterbalance or is listing to one side. This counter lean is the body's attempt to put the weight onto a joint complex (the pelvis) and reduce the muscular load.

Figure CC: Observable backwards bend with heavy objects

When an employee carries an object in one hand or two objects of different weights, it creates uneven compression on one side of the spine. This grinds the support structures of the spine together. The side-bend position also changes how the body is able to contract and utilize muscles (see fig DD). Recall that the goal is to use the largest muscles possible when applying force. When the body is put into a side-bend, it has to activate the small muscles of the spine to accommodate the load and not lose balance.

Figure DD: Side bending observed with uneven carrying

There is an additional concern with carrying an object on one shoulder. The action of lifting an object onto the shoulder requires the body to twist, no matter how carefully the lift is completed. If an employee will need to carry an object on one shoulder, such as a long piece of wood, it's best that, if possible, another team member actually places the load on the shoulder of the carrier. This allows the person who's lifting the load to stay square to the object and the person who is carrying the load to avoid the twisting motion of lifting the object onto the shoulder. The object also should not be so heavy as to make the person lean sideways to compensate (see fig EE).

Figure EE: One shoulder carry

Tool and Glove Use

Tool use is a very large component of ergonomics. When considering injury prevention, the person's ability to grip and manipulate a tool must be considered. The factors included with the assessment of tools include the size and shape of the handle, the amount of force required to activate the tool, and the tool's recoil or vibration. [28] [29]

If forceful action is required to hold or activate the tool, the person must be able to grip the tool firmly. The handle of the tool must be without protrusions, which can cause pressure areas on the hand. [30] Recall the stapler example and the idea of re-engineering the stapler with smooth edges to reduce the pressure areas on the hand. The size of the grip on a tool should be small enough so that a person can grip the handle comfortably. Lightly touch your fingers to your thumb, like the signal for okay. This is your comfortable grip size. Handles that are close to this size, but not larger than this size, will be large enough for you to grip with force. [31] Handles also should be shaped so that they do not slide in the user's hands or have areas where the user may be pinched by the tool. [32]

The lack of general maintenance for a tool often is the root cause of an injury. When a tool is not maintained, more force may need to be applied than typically necessary to activate the tool. There is a truism in the cooking world. A dull knife is more dangerous than a sharp one. This is because the forces being applied, the amount of times the forces have to be applied, and the angle at which the forces are applied change based on the lack of maintenance of the knife. Sometimes, injury prevention comes down to appropriate maintenance or selection of tools that do not require frequent maintenance, i.e., worker-proof tools.

Gloves are used to make objects easier to hold onto by increasing the friction between a handle and hand. Gloves should accomplish this without increasing forces on the muscles and joints. [33][34] Gloves are also used to protect hands from sharp objects, vibration, hot or cold objects, dirty objects, or even chemically dangerous objects. Gloves are necessary in many instances, but need to be used with caution. Gloves decrease the amount of tactile input the body receives when grasping a tool. Therefore, even though the glove provides move friction, users tend to apply more force than needed to a tool when wearing gloves than when not wearing gloves. Also, if tactile reinforcement is needed to complete the task, gloves may hinder task completion. [35] In other words, if you need to feel what is in your hand, you are more likely to put increased force into the grip or take more time and effort with the task if you are wearing gloves.

Tool vibration is also a concern if the tool is going to be used for extended periods. Hand tool vibration should be minimized whenever possible. [36] Hand-arm vibration (HAV) exposure can contribute to Raynaud's Syndrome and nerve injury. [37][38] The measurement and adaptation of tool vibration requires specific measurement devices unless the amount of vibration a tool generates is available from the tool's manufacturer. Reducing vibration is achieved with padding on the tool, better tool design, or glove use.

Chapter 15: Patient Lifting

I am including this section on patient lifting because the population with the highest rate of injury in the United States is the nursing and care professions. [39][40][41][42] The average male adult weighs around 180 pounds and with the population of the United States growing even heavier, that average is likely to increase very soon. That weight grossly exceeds the recommended lifting weight limit of 51 pounds. In addition, humans don't have handles on them to allow a good grip, the human body's weight is not evenly distributed, parts of a patient may need to be protected while being moved, such as fracture sites, the object being lifted will sometimes fight you, and the caregivers are tired. It is not surprising that caregivers report high levels of musculoskeletal injuries.

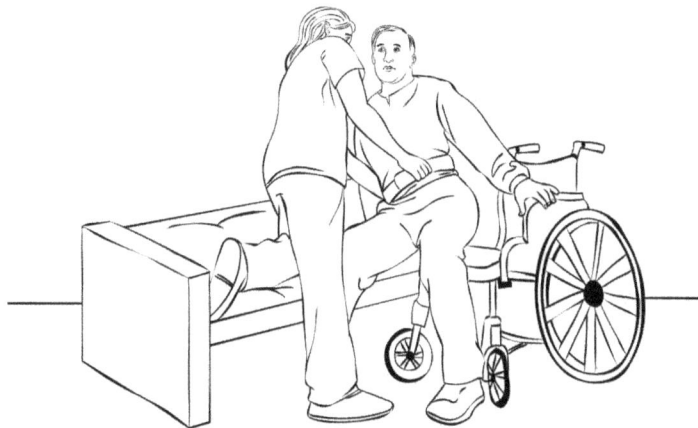

Figure FF: Patient transfers

Researchers have noted by comparison of workers' compensation data and qualitative interviews of health care providers that the caring professions have a higher injury rate than what is recorded. For example, research projects that among physical therapists—a group who should know best how to prevent injury—over 90 percent will have a work-related musculoskeletal disorder during their careers, although PTs have a very low number of reported injuries. Despite this high level of injury, physical therapists report a belief that the training they receive to be physical therapists will keep them safe even while lifting a person by themselves. [43][44]

The belief that training will keep someone safe when handling patients is false—the information I've already given you should convince you of this. There is another factor to acknowledge: When a caregiver is at risk for injury, the patient is at risk for injury. Dropping a patient because your back just gave out is a bad day at work, to say the least. Much of the funding, and therefore motivation, for patient lift devices comes from the safe patient handling advocacy and legislation focused on reducing falls in nursing and other care facilities. [45][46][47] The use of a two-person lift technique, as mentioned above, does not keep people safe. The compressive forces and sheer forces on the spine often exceed maximum allowable limits.

The good news is that there is a variety of equipment available within the hospital and nursing home environments to help protect the patient and the caregiver. This equipment includes transfer devices that can be used with patients who cannot assist with the transfer and transfer devices that allow patients to take some of the load or the entire load with a safety support. There are also ambulation devices that can be used to guard unstable patients from falling or provide lift assistance for patients who can't support their own body weight. We in the industry are simply waiting for more hospitals and nursing homes to get on the bandwagon to say no more lifting injuries and no more patient falls. Many states have passed regulations prohibiting caregivers from lifting patients; however, I have not seen a corresponding movement towards change within the care facilities.

Retrofitting a hospital or nursing home with lift equipment is much more expensive than it would have been if lift equipment had installed during construction. The cost of the equipment is a high barrier to implementation of ergonomics principles. There also is a perception among administrators and caregivers that impedes implementation, that is that the equipment will simply sit in a closet just like the other equipment already purchased.

There is one basic concept that has to be understood here. Equipment that doesn't work is not going to be used. Just as what happens in industrial plants when engineering controls are put into place without employee involvement, much of the equipment that has been purchased does not meet the expectations of the caregiver staff. Equipment that is just a few years old is bulky and requires more than one person to operate. There is also the misperception that the purpose of the equipment is to reduce the number of people needed to do a lift, i.e.,one person instead of two. However, much of the lift equipment takes two people to operate. Further, the equipment that is used as retrofit is often bulky and difficult to maneuver in hospital rooms that are getting smaller and smaller. All of these perceptions and difficulties combine to make implementation and use of lift equipment slow to be accepted and implemented.

Conclusion: The Benefits of a Good Ergonomics Program in the Industrial Setting

Industrial ergonomics is focused on eliminating hazards by first understanding them through detailed evaluation. To create effective programs, you cannot leap to conclusions about the risk factors associated with injury. A high-risk job or task must be fully evaluated before corrections can be attempted. The science of ergonomics also supplies a method of testing recommended corrections, sometimes even before they are launched or purchased.

Ergonomics programs focus on the elimination of risk areas and reduction of exposure to risks. At all times, individuals are trained to identify hazards and to protect themselves.

So what are the options for an industrial ergonomics program?

A check the box program:

> Provides some group education in the form of pre-packaged videos or classroom workshops.

This results in a low budget impact, but also a low level of effectiveness.

A good program:

> Assesses the highest risk areas and determines possible engineering, administrative, and/or behavior changes
>
> Provides customized training in a classroom

The result is a slightly more costly program, but at least it deals with the areas of greatest concerns. The training provided is more likely to be effective.

A very good program:

> Assesses the highest risk areas and determines possible engineering, administrative, and/or behavior changes
>
> Provides customized training in a classroom with time for practice. Even better, provides this on a regular basis to ensure retention and generalization
>
> Has a method for employees to report areas of concern for future evaluation
>
> Measures effectiveness through workers compensation claims and/or medical claims. Also measures effectiveness through engagement and feedback

The result is a somewhat expensive program at first, but it is more likely to show effectiveness so that further programming can be justified.

An excellent program:

- Assesses the highest risk areas and determines possible engineering, administrative, and/or behavior changes. Then moves on to the moderate risk areas, then the lower risk areas.

- Provides customized training in a classroom with practice time for current employees and new employees.

- Provides a method for employees to report areas of concern for future evaluation. Actively engages employees to continually look for "warning signs" so that areas of risk can be identified prior to the occurrence of injuries.

- Has a reminder program to reinforce change on site by taking the training on the road or into the factory so that employees are frequently reminded of the program. The program values are reinforced.

- Measures effectiveness through workers compensation claims and/or medical claims. Also measures effectiveness through engagement and feedback.

The result is a program that is expensive at first, but will have the greatest impact for the longest time period with decreasing costs corresponding to increasing reach.

As programs are developed, especially in the industrial world, it would be a shame for ergonomics to be isolated within the safety department or with the OSHA administrator. The richness of the data is something that is of greater value than the cost to gather it—if you chose to use it! This next section moves beyond the standard ergonomics programs we have been discussing and considers the other departments that may thank you for an ergonomics assessment data.

Part 5: Taking an Ergonomics Program One Step Further

So far in this book, ergonomics programming has been focused on the remediation of risk areas for a workplace. But what if I were to tell you that you could get double bang for your ergonomics buck? What if the information gathered in a traditional ergonomics assessment could be used by multiple departments, even those not involved in safety? Next, we will be talking about the idea of repurposing the data for bigger and better things.

Chapter 16: Getting Even More From Your Ergonomics Program

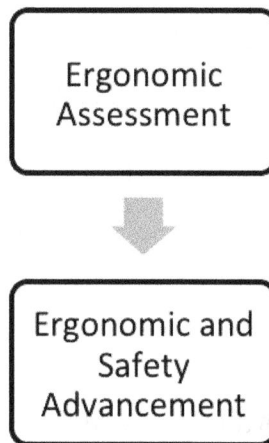

The data gathered from an ergonomics assessment is rich with information that often is overlooked but affects many aspects of an employee's work life. Traditional ergonomics programs sit in the safety or ergonomics department, and the measurements and results of analyses never get shared. However, what if you looked at the data not only as a tool to create change, but as a way to get workers back to work faster? How about if the data could even help you hire the best person for the job?

In this next section, we are going to discuss how to apply the data to some of the common documents and tests used at multiple points in the worker's job life. First, let's start with the use of ergonomics to understand the job by looking at validated job descriptions.

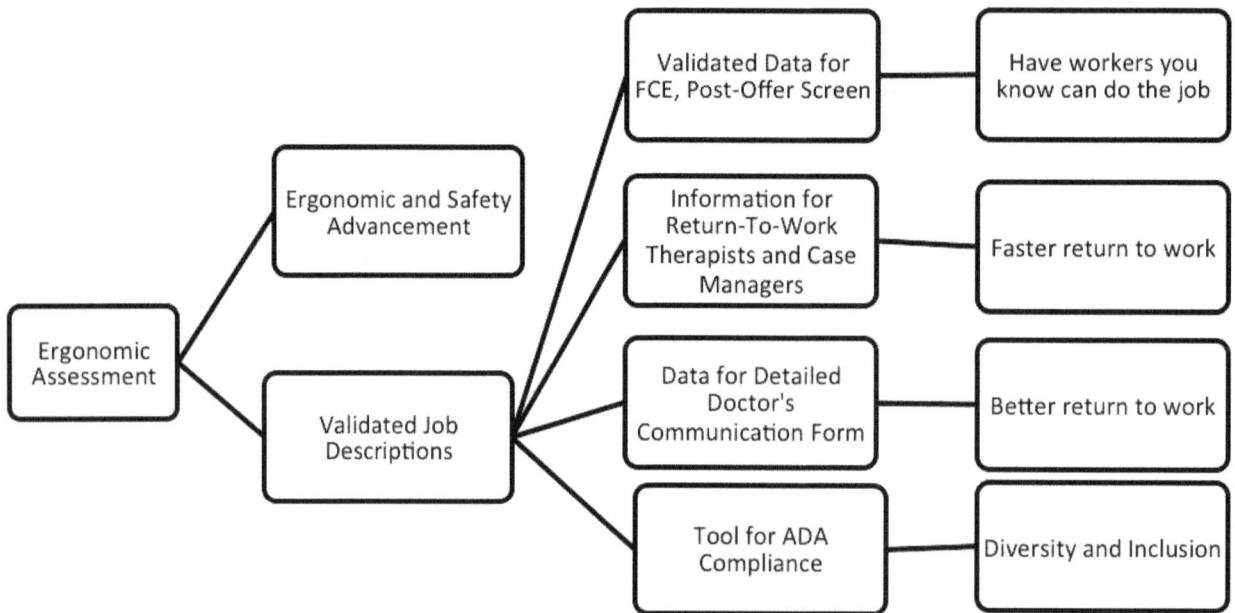

Job Descriptions

One of the things that I love about ergonomic assessment is that it doesn't need to stop at the idea of preventing injuries. Having come from the medical world before entering ergonomics, I had the chance to work on the other side of the equation—namely, treating people who had been hurt and needed to get back to work. It was there that I saw a very interesting and difficult situation. In many cases, the therapists involved in care could not identify what the employee's actual essential functions were so as to create correct goals for return to work. Very often during therapy, the goals were based on a patient's self-report of what tasks he performed at work. However, that presented a problem .Most people cannot accurately identify how they work, how much they lift and how often they lift or separate what is required versus what is habit.[48][49] Therapists who received detailed job descriptions

160

from the employer were the most successful at getting the patient back to work at a planned capacity. Unfortunately, job descriptions that were available from the company files often were not accurate or detailed.

In the current litigious environment, it is dangerous not to have detailed and validated job descriptions on file. However, many companies don't get around to making detailed job descriptions until there is a challenge to the description on file. The job descriptions that I see regularly simply state that a job is a "sedentary job" or "heavy job." The job description does not provide a detailed list of essential functions. In addition, many of the job descriptions on file now were written by a supervisor or manager, meaning that measurements may or may not have been used to create the job description. Companies often simply use the generic job descriptions available on the Occupational Information Network or O*NET (developed by a private company in conjunction with the U.S. Department of Labor). §§O*NET may be a good place to start, but the job descriptions contained there are not detailed enough to protect you from litigation or assist with directing therapy for your injured employee.

Your ergonomics program, however, provides excellent data for the development and validation of a job description. As an evaluation is completed, the ergonomics expert is documenting objective measurements of the job. While the intent of those measurements is to determine how to make the job safer, these same measurements also can be used to provide more details for a job description.

> If it is essential to the job that a person walk—they couldn't roll with a wheelchair, they couldn't crawl, or they couldn't drive—you can put in the job description that walking is essential. However, be ready to validate why bipedal walking is required, because that will come into play with

§§- *This database has replaced the Dictionary of Occupational Titles book that used to be the go-to place for generic job requirements.*

any accommodation discussion. If someone comes to you who uses a wheelchair, you have to explain why it is they could not accomplish that task in a wheelchair. You also have to be able to explain why that task cannot be accommodated to allow someone to use a wheelchair. This is not to say that your job description has to be so detailed that you take into account every modification and accommodation that could be made. Your job description should be considered a documentation tool that gives you a starting place to better understand what is actually required to do that job.

Functional job descriptions need to have careful wording to describe the details of a job. For example, if the job requires that an object is moved from one place to another, and the task does not actually require walking with the object, a job description should note that the object is "moved" not "walked." Consider the accommodations regulations described earlier in the book. Good job descriptions detail what is essential for the job in terms that generate a checklist of tasks that must be completed.

The amazing result of having a very detailed job description that has been validated—in other words, it has been tested and signed off on by employees who are experienced in that job—is that the document becomes a tool that can be used to create other documents of very high value. For example, one of the biggest challenges of getting someone back to work after an injury is the doctor's note of limitations. Typically, doctors are given a very generic form on which they fill out how much a person can lift, how far they can walk, whether they can stand for long periods of time, and other basic information. What the ergonomics assessment allows you to do with your job description is create a checklist of what the person actually *must* do. The doctor would be able to detail the employee's limitations. The therapist can now direct treatment towards specific work related goals to improve those abilities. Therefore, you get to your employee back to work faster and reduce your losses due to absences, replacement, and medical fees.

Let's look at how this might play out:

You have an employee who works on a manufacturing floor and whose job is to monitor the production line. We will call her Chandra. The company's original job description says this job is a "sedentary job." The original doctor's note asks: Can Chandra return to a "sedentary job?" Now, Chandra broke her pelvis and cannot sit for long periods of time due to pain. There is nothing wrong with her eyes and there is nothing wrong with her brain. The doctor takes a look at the note and it says "sedentary." The word "sedentary" brings to mind sitting all day, although in truth, standing all day is also considered "sedentary" in the world of ergonomics. The doctor signs: No, Chandra cannot return to work.

A revised job description that includes details says that the essential function of the job is to monitor a board and video screen and look through a window. This job description states the job can be completed sitting or standing—the essential function is the ability to identify problems on the assembly line. The doctor's form is modified and asks: Can Chandra return to a job where she must monitor a board and video screen and look through a window? The form states that the job can be completed seated or standing. The doctor now can release Chandra for return to work four hours a day with the option to sit and stand as needed.

Research demonstrates that it is very important to return injured workers to work in less than six months in order to have a greater chance of getting them back to work at all. If injured employees are out of work for six months or more, the likelihood of their return to work is reduced. Therefore, it is best to get your employees back as soon as possible in whatever position or role is available to keep the employee engaged in work behavior. Now, Chandra was a very simplified example. Return to work is complicated by multiple factors other than whether the employee can complete the essential functions of the job, such as whether the person is able to travel to work or is on pain medication that may limit alertness. But I hope this gives you a starting point for understanding how job description can benefit from the integration of information from ergonomic assessments.

Functional Capacity Evaluations

Functional capacity evaluations or FCEs, also known as *functional job testing, fit testing, post-offer screens*, and *post-offer evaluations*, are a measurement tool to assess how well a worker can complete the job requirements. The worker is put through a series of work tasks, either simulated or on a safe job site. An evaluator who has been trained to complete FCEs assesses how many of the essential functions the worker can do safely in full or in part. The tasks included in the assessment must accurately represent what the employee would need to do on the job. This is another place for you to get further return on your ergonomics investment.

The ergonomics assessment includes a professional measurement of essential job functions. As discussed above, you already have converted the data into a detailed job description. The biggest challenge facing employers today is validating the FCE. Discrepancies between the job and the test are one reason why FCEs are challenged during lawsuits involving workers' compensation. The company must ensure that the jobs tested reflect the jobs done. With a detailed job description supported by an ergonomics assessment, the FCE now has objective measurements supporting the jobs tested. If the testing parameters accurately reflect what is on the ergonomics assessment and validated job description, there is less room for discrepancy. The most accurate functional capacity evaluations are created from full job evaluations. An ergonomics assessment may not give you a full analysis of all of the job tasks; however, the ergonomics expert can be asked to expand his tests to include all essential functions. After all, the ergonomics expert already will be with the employees for extended periods of time to measure various components of the job.

So what does an FCE look like?

During a test of functional abilities, the employee, Mason, will be asked to simulate portions of a job task. For safety reasons, the evaluator often starts by having the employee do an activity that is not as heavy as what is required on the job. For example, if the job requires the employee to move a 40 pound bag 20 feet on a level, even surface, the evaluator may start Mason with a 10 pound bag carried for 20 feet. Once Mason demonstrates the ability to carry the lighter amount for 20 feet, the evaluator will ask Mason to move up the challenge in small increments.

If the FCE does not accurately reflect the job tasks, the evaluator could test and fail Mason erroneously. Let's say Mason works his way up with well performed 20, 30, and 40 pound lifts and is finally asked to lift 50 pounds because the evaluator does not have an accurate and detailed job description. The evaluator only knows that the job is listed as "moderately heavy." However, in reality, the job only requires a 40 pound lift. This is still correctly called "moderately heavy." Mason stops the test, perhaps due to fatigue, and does not show the capability to lift 50 pounds. If the evaluator documents that Mason was not able to meet the job level of "moderately heavy," can Mason 'fail' the FCE and be denied return to work based on the test parameters? I would not recommend denying Mason the opportunity to return to work based on this FCE. The test was invalid; Mason should not have been asked to lift 50 pounds, and the conclusions from the results are therefore invalid.

It is common for FCEs to be used after an employee is injured as an assessment for return to work. The same test, however, can be used to measure the ability of new hires to complete the job requirements prior to even starting the job. The name of the test changes to a *post-offer screen* or *pre-employment screen*. In both versions of the FCE, as a return to work tool or a post-offer tool, functional capacity evaluations have been hotly contested in the court system. Again, the primary component to remember when designing these tools or using the data from these tools is whether the measurements taken during the test have been validated to assure that they relate directly to the tasks involved in the work. The majority of the complaints where the court system found in favor of the employee occurred when the FCE components assessed could not be verified as directly related to the applicable job.

Post-offer screens or pre-employment screens are done after the person has been offered the job. Consider these screens in the same category as drug testing and background testing. The applicant/new hire, Joseph, is tested to see if he has the ability to complete the essential job functions prior to completing employment processing. Instead of a formal test, some companies simply use the first few weeks or few months of employment as a probationary period to assess whether this person can complete the job tasks. This probationary method, however, places a person in a state of potential risk. The company is putting a new employee on the job when it is not known whether the person is physically capable of completing the job without injury. As much as ergonomics attempts to make jobs safe for the average individual using general normative data, there is no guarantee that this applicant fits the capabilities of "normal." Just because a job only requires a manageable and safe lift, is not to say that every person can complete that lift.

So, if Joseph fails a pre-employment screen, there are a variety of next steps available for him and the company. Joseph could be encouraged to participate in a program that would build his strength to allow him to complete the job required. He could be denied the job outright. Joseph could be asked to move into a job that better meets his tested abilities. Or, if possible, the job could be modified to meet Josephs' abilities.

If Joseph failed the test, in essence he has shown on a test that he cannot actually complete the job as currently defined *safely*. Let's say that Joseph goes out on the job while you're getting all of your data together and completes all of the job tasks for a week. Who is right:the assessment or Joseph? In truth, both the employee and the evaluator are correct. Employees often can complete a job using compensatory movements that are not necessarily safe. If the tasks were completed in an unsafe manner, the evaluator would have scored the tasks as *not completed safely* or as *fail*. Joseph may be able to complete the job tasks, but he is at high risk for injury.

The convoluted nature of post-offer screenings is one of the reasons these tests are not used often unless the job is specialized, such as with emergency responders. On the other hand, the use of a post-offer screening test takes away the potential for being accused of discrimination. Everyone who applies is given the test regardless of gender, size, color, or reported ability. The screen is a tool to assess ability without the influence of the person's characteristics.

A company should never use a pre-made or pre-packaged functional capacity evaluation without validating it with the company's actual job. There are number of pre-made FCEs on the market, and I highly recommend that you ask your attorney to take a look at one before you seriously consider it. There have been a number of cases where such pre-made evaluations have been shown to be inaccurate and invalid for the job in question. It could be as simple as the evaluation itself has too short a testing time period. The evaluation tested an employee for two hours, but the job requires eight hours. Can a two-hour test accurately demonstrate if an employee would be able to tolerate a full eight hours?

Unfortunately, there is conflicting data in the research as to how long someone should be tested in order to assess an eight-hour day. For example, many of these out-of-the-box evaluation tools are two to four hours a day for one or two days. The test designers have done studies and have shown that the four-hour test accurately represents jobs for eight hours a day. Studies not done by test designers disagree at times and agree at other times with the conclusion that a shorter time period is all that is needed. I will not go into the case history here, as much of it will depend on your state and your regulatory boards.

I can tell you that I will no longer perform out-of-the-box evaluations. I decided after reading the history of various court rulings and the research available about extrapolating data, that I simply would not feel comfortable enough with the accuracy of my conclusions to sign off on a pre-made form. The best evaluations I've seen, that have held up in court time and time again, are evaluations that take place in the same environment as the job itself and use situations and tools specific to that job. Customized and realistic evaluations are expensive. The cost often is only justified for jobs that are very high risk.

I recommend using caution when working with an FCE designer or workers' compensation case manager regarding the validity of the test itself, and discussing with your attorneys what your particular state's history is regarding functional capacity evaluation legislation. Each state has a different policy and a different history within the court system.

Part 6: Who Plays in The Ergonomics Sandbox?

Chapter 17: Shopping for Ergonomics Experts

To help you become better consumers, I have summarized below some of the professionals you will encounter in the ergonomics programming world. This section does come with a bit of a disclaimer: Yes, this is what I do for a living. I'm going to do my best to give you information on the various professionals that work in this field in the most objective way. I have attempted to mute any personal bias so that you can make an informed decision for yourself. I have to generalize quite a bit in the section because I don't know what any particular individual has done to continue his education. It is quite possible that a person with a specific professional designation has completed additional training to become an expert in ergonomics even though the professional field itself does not include sufficient training for its professionals to be considered, in my mind, ergonomics experts.

A good barometer for whether you want to work with a given professional is to examine how the professional makes money. The majority of consultants who work in ergonomics as their profession make money based on expertise—they sell you their time and their knowledge. Other professionals provide ergonomic services for free and make their money from either pulling your employees into their clinic for services or by selling you equipment. You can decide with which type you'd prefer to work.

The best way to find a good ergonomics expert is to ask your peers for referrals. Speak to other HR professionals in your specific industry. Many professionals in this field work outside of their own geographic area ¶¶ because of the portability of knowledge. You are not limited to a company or individual who is based in your

---

¶¶- *My own company is based in Maryland, but I travel around the world working in ergonomics and provide services remotely to all sections of the globe. It is important to determine what you need for your program before deciding to limit your search geographically.*

geographic region. The number of resources available to you is limited only by funding. This is the main reason I recommend relying on referrals.

Medical Professionals

Just about every medical professional can be found in the world of ergonomics. Most common are the professionals who work in rehabilitation or occupational medicine. Within the field of medicine, it is rare to have a school of medicine that focuses on ergonomics anywhere in the curriculum. Medical professionals, if they choose to work in ergonomics, often have obtained additional information and training. Unless otherwise noted, I personally would consider the professionals listed here as ergonomics experts only if they had additional training specifically in ergonomics.

Chiropractors: This is a form of alternative medicine that focuses on the treatment of musculoskeletal problems most often through manipulation, exercise, and some use of orthotics. Some chiropractic schools include an introduction to ergonomics.

Medical doctors (MD or DO): The field of medicine and doctors is varied. There are a number of subspecialties within medicine that specifically focus on the workforce.

> **General practitioners** (GP): I feel it's important to mention your employee's personal physician in this section because, although the GP does not get involved in ergonomics at the worksite, GPs are often called upon by the employee for information on how to deal with conditions that the employee associates with the workplace. GPs do not typically have any additional training in ergonomics or the workplace.

> **Occupational medicine physicians**: The primary role of physicians who specialize in occupational medicine is to evaluate the interaction between work and health. These are medical doctors who have chosen to continue

their education specifically within the field of work. Occupational medicine physicians often work inside of a company to help protect worker health and have some basic training in ergonomics.

Physiatrists: Physical medicine and rehabilitation physicians have specialty training in how medicine works with rehabilitation in various forms. These are medical doctors who often are used when conservative methods are needed and surgery is not recommended. They are specialists in understanding how all the rehabilitative fields work together. Physiatrists often do not get involved in ergonomics, but instead are found within the world of independent medical evaluations, functional capacity evaluations, and return to work.

Occupational therapists: OT is a field focused on how a person is able to complete everyday activities. Occupational therapy is not focused solely on the musculoskeletal and nervous systems; it also addresses sensory systems, and cognition as well as psychosocial, cultural, and other components of a person to assist them in completing their everyday activities. OT schools typically include ergonomics training under the topics of joint protection and energy conservation.

Physical therapists: PT is a field focused on how the body moves and functions as a connected unit, focusing on the musculoskeletal and nervous systems. PT schools typically include an introduction to ergonomics.

> There is often confusion between physical therapy and occupational therapy. In general, PTs focus on the physical whereas OTs focus on any component limiting the person's ability to work, play, dress, etc. I sometimes explain to my patients that physical therapists will help you get from point A to point B. Occupational therapists will help you with everything you want to do when you get to point B.

Psychology: **Psychologists** and **psychiatrists** will get involved in the workplace in various forms. They can be involved in evaluating stress related to the workplace. They often are involved in research about workplace stressors, including environmental stressors and psychosocial stressors. Also, they may choose to specialize in industrial psychology. Their scholastic training does not typically include ergonomics.

Industrial/organizational psychology: This is a branch of psychology that focuses on the study of how workplaces and individuals affect each other, and psychologists and physiatrists who focus on this subspecialty study the individual factors related to workplace issues such as teamwork and organization. They are a resource for the behavioral change or contextual feature that may affect how people behave safely or unsafely.

Engineering

The field of engineering is very broad, with the majority of engineers having a subspecialty or focus. Engineers who choose to continue and focus on ergonomics can either call themselves engineers or take on a more specialized nomenclature.

Industrial engineers: This branch of engineering deals with optimizing complex processes. These engineers look at how to make a system function with less waste, including time, money, man-hours, energy, and other resources. Industrial engineers often get involved in ergonomics because, as we mentioned, ergonomics is a method of reducing waste—whether that is wasting somebody's energy or wearing out employees so that they cannot continue to work.

Human factor engineers: This is a branch of engineering and psychology that looks at how a human functions both in strengths and weaknesses and applies those strengths and weakness to the design of technology. Human factors engineering often is used as a synonym for ergonomics. Departments of study may list ergonomics as "human factors and ergonomics."

System engineering: These are engineers who specialize in improving and creating efficient systems. System engineers often get involved in ergonomics because risk management is within their wheelhouse.

An interesting aspect of ergonomics is that professionals can come from a wide variety of fields and continue their education to specialize in some facet of ergonomics, whether that is physical ergonomics, cognitive ergonomics, or organizational ergonomics, all of which are sub-specialties within the world of ergonomics. You may encounter someone who practices in ergonomics from a field not listed above. There are a number of certifications and, shall we say, letters behind the name, that can give you a clue as to how much continuing education or effort the person has made to become a specialist in ergonomics. However, it is important to note that many experts do not have any of these letters. Unfortunately, as with many fields, those letters are not sufficient to be sure that the person is actually good at their job.

Chapter 18: Certifications

All of the following certificates are trademarked.

Board Certified Professional Ergonomist (BCPE or CPE): This is an internationally recognized certification administered by third party (not a school or for-profit organization). It is common for industrial companies to request that the ergonomics expert have this certification. However, not everyone who works in the field sits for the certification exam, as it is both expensive and based on engineering principles. People who are not from the engineering field require additional training and classes before they can sit for this exam regardless of their previous ergonomics experience.

Certified Ergonomic Assessment Specialist (CEAS): This is a certification granted by a training company, the Back School of Atlanta, who provides both the training and the exam. This is a common method for people who do not have an engineering background to get certification letters.

Certified Ergonomic Evaluation Specialist (CEES): A certification issued by the Matheson Group, who provides continuing education and testing. This is another common method for people who do not have an engineering background to get certification letters.

Certified Safety Professional (CSP): This is a national certification that comes in various formats specific to what the person plans on doing and the person's professional background. This is a certification based on exam. Individuals with this certification have training in safety and have learned some of the basics of ergonomics, but ergonomics is not a focus on the exam.

When you develop an ergonomics program, it is important to know what you want to get out of it and what you're willing to put into it. Find a professional who provides you a pathway to meeting the company's goals. Ask for references and ask your peers for recommendations, but even more importantly, meet with the professional and decide if you are satisfied with their knowledge. You are now a pretty savvy shopper!

Conclusion: Ergonomics Makes Good Sense and Cents:

If you have read through this book, I hope you now have a good idea of the basics of ergonomics, how to organize and prioritize your ergonomics program, and what ergonomics program components work or don't work according to the research.

Ergonomics programs give you return on investment as soon as you implement them. Just giving your employees the knowledge that your company cares about their safety and health has been shown to increase employees' positive feelings about their jobs. Being heard and being a part of a solution is extremely important to employees' job satisfaction.

An ergonomics program can cost a lot in the beginning if you choose to truly address the problems. Even if you choose to do the bare minimum, understanding how to get the most from those beginning dollars will help your program grow and succeed. Where is your company on the spectrum of safety and preventing injuries? Do you need to be reactive to injuries that are already being reported? Do you need to have a broader approach and address as many people as possible before diving deep into problem areas? Many professionals will help you develop your ergonomics program after conducting a needs assessment. You don't have to do this by yourself, but even more importantly, I hope that you now have sufficient information to feel confident that you will be a good consumer of ergonomics professional services.

Afterword: Where to Go From Here?

There are a number of resources available for more in-depth information on specific concepts discussed in this book. I've listed many of them at the end of this chapter. I believe that one of the purposes of an expert in the field is to help you find information and give you easily understood solutions. From writing previous books, I have realized that it is impossible for me to answer every single question that may come up. Please feel free to consider me a resource. If you have a question that has not been addressed in this book, you can email me at naomi@workinjuryfree.com.

Appendix A: Additional resources

OSHA

Osha.gov

NIOSH

Cdc.gov/niosh

NIOSH Total Worker Health Program

Cdc.gov/niosh/twh

Human Factors and Ergonomic Society

hfes.org

Board Certification of Professional Ergonomists

bcpe.org

American Industrial Hygiene Association

aiha.org

American Society of Safety Engineers

asse.org

International Ergonomics Association

iea.cc

Chesapeake Region Safety Council (local)

chesapeakesc.org

Business and Institutional Furniture Manufacturer's Association

bifma.org

Appendix B: Measurement Tools in Industrial Ergonomics

Below is a summary of the four most common ergonomic assessment tools that you will come across. These are:

The NIOSH Lifting Equation

Snook and Cirello Tables aka Liberty Mutual Tables

Rapid Upper Limb Assessment (RULA)

Rapid Entire Body Assessment (REBA)

NIOSH Lifting Equation

The **NIOSH Lifting Equation** is from the National Institute of Safety and Health, a part of the Center for Disease Control (CDC). The equation is a guideline that OSHA strongly suggests you follow, but it is not enforced by legal regulations. The NIOSH Lifting Equation is used to analyze how safe a lift is for the lifter's back. To analyze other body parts, such as the arms and wrists, an additional assessment will be required.

The lifting equation is used to analyze **two-handed** lifting and lowering tasks.

Measures are taken at the beginning and end of the lift to determine where the object being lifted is in space (how high off the ground and how far from the body), how easy it is to grab (handles or no handles), how much the person twists while retrieving and placing the object, and how frequently the object is moved (number of times per minute for how many hours per day). The weight of the object is also measured.

The outputs from the NIOSH Lifting Equation are the **Recommended Weight Limit** (RWL) and **Lifting Index** (LI). The RWL is how much 75% of women and 99% of men can lift safely based on the conditions entered (the maximum the object should weigh based on where it is in space and where it is moved). The LI tells you how close the real weight is relative to how much it should weigh (the RWL) in these conditions for both the lift and the lower.

A way to think about this equation is to consider that we know that people can lift 51 pounds one time safely if it is close to the body without twisting and the lifter has a good grip on it. Each measurement you take will chip away at the 51 pounds until you get the recommended weight limit.

The equation result is a score of green, yellow, or red.

- If your LI is less than 1, you are lifting less than a safe value so you are green or "good to go."

- If your LI is between 1.0 and 3.0, you are lifting more than you should; that lift is considered a concern, but not an emergency, scored "yellow".

- When your LI is higher than 3.0, you are lifting more than 3 times the recommended weight and there is a definite need for improvement, or red score.

A yellow or red score is cause for concern. With these scores, it is best to make an effort to reduce the risk factors. Another use for the NIOSH equation is to change one or more features of the lift and evaluate how much change will occur. For example, if the lift scored moderate risk, or yellow, you could lower the amount of weight being lifted to reduce the risk. By using the new weight as a new input into the equation, you can see if changing the weight will reduce the risk to green.

The NIOSH Lifting Equation is very complicated when written down, but it's quite simple to conduct an assessment once you are familiar with what measurements to take. Just remember it is only accurate a predicting low back pain for two-handed lifting/lowering tasks. It does not take into account any movements done between the lift portion and the lower portion. If the employee lifts a box from a table, dances a waltz, and then puts the box back on the table, the NIOSH equation will only "see" the box on the table twice.

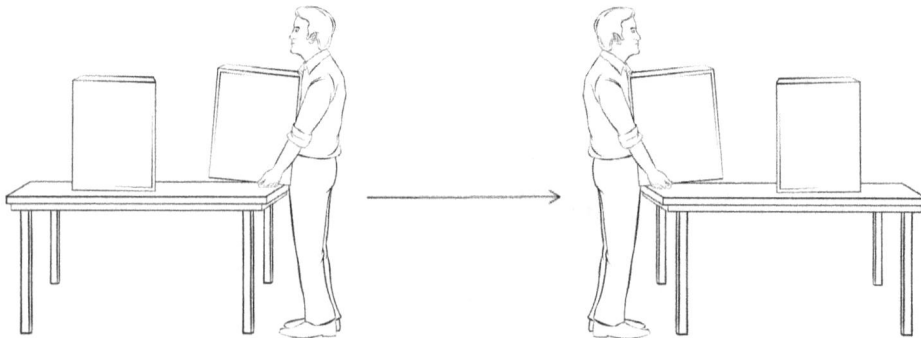

> This equation does not account for anything that happens between the lift and lower.

This equation cannot take into account what happens if the person is using a long handled tool with the weight at the end, like when using a shovel.

Snook and Cirello Tables, aka Liberty Mutual Tables

Snook and Cirello Tables, aka Liberty Mutual Tables (named for their creators and now the company that publishes the data), are used to analyze pushing, pulling, lifting and carrying tasks. The data gathered were mainly based on physical and psychophysical measurements. Psychophysical measures are measures of what a person thinks he can physically do. For example, it is a measure of how much weight a person *thinks* he can lift X number of times in Y number of hours with W height handles and how much weight he can *actually* lift in these same conditions. The tables are quite simple to use, but contain only limited data. If the exact conditions you need aren't available, you will need to extrapolate between two data sets.

To use the tables, first determine the population for whom you are designing. If you are designing a manufacturing plant and trying to figure out how far away you can put a button, it is recommended to use a smaller-framed person as your model, that is, if this person can reach the button, then everyone else should be able to reach the button. Therefore, you would look at the chart columns related to 75 percent of the female population in order to see what the majority of the typically smaller population (females) can do. Once a population is selected, you can locate the relevant information on the chart.

If we consider the push/pull charts, for example, the table will list how much the population (female, 75%) can push or pull at 20 inches from the floor for both initial force and sustained force. The initial force is how much force is acceptable to get a cart moving. The sustained force is how much force is needed to keep the cart moving when traveling, such as across the plant or office.

The push/pull numbers from the chart need to be compared to the forces measured in the field with a push/pull dynamometer. It is important to ascertain that you are addressing the hardest part of the job. It is recommended that, during a field assessment, the evaluator ensures that the worst case scenario is taken into account, such as starting the push when the wheel is behind a divot on the floor. When measuring the sustained push forces needed with the push/pull dynamometer, again, it is best to ensure the worst case scenario is taken into account, such as pushing up a ramp on the production floor.

Unlike the push/pull tables, the tables that describe carrying only reference the recommended weight as related to the distance traveled and the dimensions of

181

the lift. In other words, if I have to carry something 20 feet, how heavy can the object be? The tables do not take into account details, such as the grip on the object being carried or the method used to pick up or put down the object. Instead, a comparison of the lifting table and the carrying table would need to be completed to understand the full risks of a task. If we analyzed a task such as moving a box onto a storage rack, we would need to compare three tables:

- Pick up the box from the floor = use the table on lifting objects floor to carrying height

- Carry the box to the storeroom = use the table on carrying objects

- Put the box on the shelf = use the table of lifting objects from carrying height to shoulder height

These three numbers would be compared and the lowest weight value selected to ensure that the task was safe. By selecting the lowest weight value, you are ensuring that the hardest portion of the task can be completed. For example, consider these maximum safe weights for each portion:

- Pick up the box: 20 pounds

- Carry the box: 25 pounds

- Put the box on the shelf: 15 pounds

You would need to limit the weight of the object to 15 pounds so that the entire task is safe.

The Snook and Cirello tables are the easiest of all assessment tools to use, especially in electronic form that has drop down menus. The main limitation of these tables is the limited amount of data available. Also, like the NIOSH Lifting Equation, the Snook and Cirello tables are predictors of low back pain, not injuries of any other body parts.

Vibration

Vibration assessments can be done in two ways. There are both hand-arm vibration and whole-body vibration assessment tools. Both assessment tools require the use of an accelerometer to measure the exposure to vibration. The American Conference of Governmental Industrial Hygienists (ACGIH) have developed **Threshold Limit Values** (TLVs) that represent acceptable limits for vibration exposure. When vibration is measured, it is measured in terms of an eight-hour equivalent exposure. Hand-arm vibration exposure should stay below 5 m/s^2 to minimize the risk of white finger syndrome or Raynoud's Syndrome, a decrease in circulation and/or nerve damage to the hands and feet. Instead of flat number limit, whole body vibration exposure is judged on a curve based on exposure. Vibration is easy to measure, but accelerometers and the computer needed to analyze the data are expensive.

Rapid Upper Limb Assessment

Rapid Upper Limb Assessment (RULA) is an assessment tool that focuses on posture and is used to estimate the risk of upper limb disorders. A RULA is a quick and systematic way to look at the postural risks of a worker who works primarily using her arms and hands. When using the RULA, the assessor will watch a worker or take video of the worker. The evaluator then measures the upper arm postures, such as the shoulder position, i.e., angle of the upper arm in relation to the back, the angle of the elbow, the angle of the wrist, whether the wrist is twisting, and the forces/load applied. Once these measurements are taken, scores are calculated using a simple table and then added together for a final risk score for the arms and wrists.

In addition to the arms, the RULA looks at the neck and trunk/back postures as they relate to the arm positions. The final RULA score is a combination of all of the upper limb scores. If the score is 1 or 2, it is considered acceptable. A score of 3 or 4 denotes that the task needs further investigation. For scores of 5 or 6, further investigation and solution implementations are needed soon. And finally, a score of 7 means that a change should be investigated and implemented immediately.

Rapid Entire Body Assessment

Rapid Entire Body Assessment (REBA) is used for a quick analysis of the entire body. Similar to the RULA, the REBA looks at body part angles only. The first part of the REBA assesses the neck, trunk/back, leg postures, and the forces/loads applied and concludes with a score of risk. The second score is gathered from the arm and wrist postures, similar to the RULA. These two scores are then combined to get a final REBA score. If the final score is 1, there is negligible risk. For a score of 2 or 3, the risk is considered low. With a score of 4 to 7, the risk is medium and further investigation is needed. Scores of 8 to 10 equate to high risk, and scores of 11 or above are considered very high risk. In general, scores above 8 should have a change investigated and implemented immediately.

Notes

1 International Ergonomics Association. (2000). Definition of ergonomics. Retrieved from http://www.iea.cc/01_what/What%20is%20Ergonomics.html

2 Bernard, B. P. (Ed.). (1997). Musculoskeletal disorders and workplace factors: A critical review of epidemiologic evidence for work-related musculoskeletal disorders of the neck, upper extremity, and low back. Washington, DC: U.S. Department of Health and Human Services National Institute for Occupational Safety and Health.

3 Kingma, I., Faber, G. S., & van Dieen, J. (2010). How to lift a box that is too large to fit between the knees. Ergonomics, 53(10), 1228-1238.

4 Garg, A., & Hegmann, K. (2006). Applied ergonomics: Low back. Milwaukee, WI: University of Wisconsin_Milwaukee.

5 Kingma, I., Faber, G. S., & van Dieen, J. (2010). How to lift a box that is too large to fit between the knees. Ergonomics, 53(10), 1228-1238.

6 Garg, A., & Hegmann, K. (2006). Applied ergonomics: Low back. Milwaukee, WI: University of Wisconsin_Milwaukee.

7 Chapman, A. E. (2008). Biomechanical analysis of fundamental human movements. Champaign, IL: Human Kinetics.

8 Braveman, B., & Page, J. J. (Eds.). (2012). Work: Promoting participation and productivity through occupational therapy. Philadelphia, PA: F.A. Davis Company.

9 Chapman, A. E. (2008). Biomechanical analysis of fundamental human movements. Champaign, IL: Human Kinetics.

10 Sanders, M. S., & McCormick, E. J. (1976). Human Factors in Engineering and Design (7th ed.). New York: McGraw-Hill, Inc.

11 US Department of Labor. (2004). OSHA forms for recording work-related injuries and illnesses. Retrieved 2012, from http://www.osha.gov/recordkeeping/new-osha300form1-1-04.pdf

12 Ibid, 2004

13 Chapman, A. E. (2008). Biomechanical analysis of fundamental human movements. Champaign, IL: Human Kinetics.

14 NIOSH. (2007, April 27). Nonfatal occupational injuries and illnesses -- United States 2004. MMWR Weekly. Retrieved August 2012, from http://www.cdc.gov/mmwr/preview/ mmwrhtml/mm5616a3.htm

15 Luttmann, A., Jager, M., & Griefahn, B. (n.d.). Protecting workers' health series no. 5: Preventing musculoskeletal disorders in the workplace. World Health Organization.

16 NIOSH, 2007

17 Luttmann, n.d.

18 Bureau of Labor Statistics. (2011, November 9). News release: Nonfatal occupational injuries and illnesses requiring days away from work, 2010. Retrieved August 2012, from http://www.bls.gov/news.release/pdf/osh2.pdf

19 Ogden, C. L., Carroll, M. D., Kit, B. K., & Flegal, K. M. (2012). Prevalence of obesity in the United States, 2009-1010. NCHS data brief, no 82. Hyattsville, MD: National Center for Health Statistics.

20 Thornton, A. (2011). Sleep apnea: What employers should know. The American Sleep Apnea Association. Retrieved 2012, from http://www.sleepapnea.org/asaa-blog/sleep-apnea-what-every-employer-should-know.html

21 Delisle, A., Lariviere, C., Plamondon, A., & Imbeau, D. (2006). Comparison of three computer office workstations offering forearm support: Impact on upper limb posture and muscle activation. Ergonomics, 49(2), 139-160.

22 Bernard, B. P. (Ed.). (1997). Musculoskeletal disorders and workplace factors: A critical review of epidemiologic evidence for work-related musculoskeletal disorders of the neck, upper extremity, and low back. Washington, DC: U.S. Department of Health and Human Services, National Institute for Occupational Safety and Health.

23 Ramazzini, B. (1940). Diseases of workers (Latin) (W. C. Wright, Trans.). Chicago, IL: University of Chicago Press. (Original work published 1700) found quoted in Pronk, N.P. (July, 2015). Design recommendations for active workplaces. Ergonomics in Design. Erg.sagepub.com DOI: 10.1177/1064804615585408. Human Factors and Ergonomics Society, July 21, 2015

24 Loffler, D., Wallmann-Sperlich, B., Wan, J., Knott, J., Vogel, A., & Hurtienne, J. (July, 2015). Office ergonomics driven by contextual design. Ergonomics in Design. Erg. sagepub.com DOI: 10.1177/1064804615585409. Human Factors and Ergonomics Society, July 21, 2015

25 John, D., Lyden, K., & Bassett, D. (July 2015) A physiological perspective on treadmill and sit-to-stand workstations. Erg.sagepub.com DOI: 10.1177/1064804615585411. Human Factors and Ergonomics Society, July 21, 2015

26 Garg, A., & Hegmann, K. (2006). Applied ergonomics: Low back. Milwaukee, WI: University of Wisconsin_Milwaukee.

27 Chapman, A. E. (2008). Biomechanical analysis of fundamental human movements. Champaign, IL: Human Kinetics.

28 Sanders, M. S., & McCormick, E. J. (1976). Human Factors in Engineering and Design (7th ed.). New York: McGraw-Hill, Inc.

29 Woodson, W. E., Tillman, B., & Tillman, P. (1992). Human factors design handbook (2nd ed.). New York: McGraw-Hill, Inc.

30 Sanders, 1976

31 Chapman, 2008

32 Woodson, et al, 1992

33 Chapman, 2008

34 Sanders et al, 1976

35 Ibid, 1976

36 Bernard, 1997

37 Sanders et al., 1976

38 Woodson, et al., 1992

39 Barnes, A. F. (2007). Erasing the word 'lift' from nurses' vocabulary when handling patients. British Journal of Nursing, 16(18), 1144-1147.

40 Keller, S. (2009). Effects of extended work shifts and shift work on patient safety, productivity, and employee health. American Association of Occupational Health Nurses Journal, 57(12), 497-502.

41 Marras, W. S., Davis, K. G., Kirking, B. C., & Bertsche, P. K. (1999). A comprehensive analysis of low-back disorder risk and spinal loading during the transferring and repositioning of patients using different techniques. Ergonomics, 42(7), 904-926.

42 Nelso, A., Matz, M., Chen, F., Siddarthan, K., Lloyd, J., & Fragala, G. (2006). Development and evaluation of a multifaceted ergonomics program to prevent injuries associated with patient handling tasks. International Journal of Nursing Studies, 43, 717-733.

43 Cromie, J. E., Robertson, J. E., & Best, M. O. (2002). Work-related musculoskeletal disorders and the culture of physical therapy. Physical Therapy, 82, 459-472.

44 Cromie, J. E., Robertson, V. J., & Best, M. O. (2000). Work-related musculoskeletal disorders in physical therapists: prevalence, severity, risks, and responses. Physical Therapy, 80, 336-351.

45 Barnes, 2007

46 Collins et al., 2006

47 Collins et al., 2004

48 Grandy, M. S., & Westwood, D. A. (2006). Opposite perceptual and sensorimotor Responses to a size-weight illusion. Journal of Neurophysiology, 95, 3887-3892.

49 Naylor, Y. K., & Amazeen, E. L. (2004). The size-weight illusion in team lifting. Human Factors: The Journal of the Human Factors and Ergonomics Society, 46, 349-356.

Bibliography

Abrams, N. (2011). *Occupation-Based Office Ergonomics.* Rockville: NAOE Publishing.

Baker, N. A. (2009). Alternative keyboards. *Work & Industry Special Interest Section Quarterly, 23*(3), pp. 1-4.

Baker, N. A., & Cidboy, E. L. (2006). The effect of three alternative keyboard designs on forearm pronation, wrist extension, and ulnar deviation: A meta-analysis. *American Journal of Occupational Therapy, 60*(1), 40-79.

Baker, N. A., & Redfern, M. (2009). Potentially problematic postures during work site keyboard use. *The American Journal of Occupational Therapy, 63*(4), 386-397.

Barnes, A. F. (2007). Erasing the word 'lift' from nurses' vocabulary when handling patients. *British Journal of Nursing, 16*(18), 1144-1147.

Bernard, B. P. (Ed.). (1997). Musculoskeletal disorders and workplace factors: A critical review of epidemiologic evidence for work-related musculoskeletal disorders of the neck, upper extremity, and low back. Washington, DC: U.S. Department of Health and Human Services ,National Institute for Occupational Safety and Health.

Bongers, P. M., Ijmker, S., van den Heuvel, S., & Blatter, B. M. (2006). Epidemiology of work related neck and upper limb problems: Psychsocial and personal risk factors (Part I) and effective interventions from a bio behavioural perspective (Part II). *Journal of Occupational Rehabilitation, 16*, 279-302.

Braveman, B., & Page, J. J. (Eds.). (2012). *Work: Promoting particpation and productivity through occupational therapy.* Philidelphia, PA: F.A. Davis Company.

Brewer, S., Van Eerd, D., Amick III, B. C., Irvin, E., Daum, K. M., Gerr, F., . . . Rempel, D. (2006). Workplace interventions to prevent musculoskeletal and visual symptoms and disorders among computer users: A systematic review. *Journal of Occupational Rehabilitation*, 16, 325-358.

Bureau of Labor Statistics. (2011, November 9). News release: Nonfatal occupational injuries and illnesses requiring days away from work, 2010. Retrieved August 2012, from http://www.bls.gov/news.release/pdf/osh2.pdf

Chapman, A. E. (2008). *Biomechanical analysis of fundamental human movements.* Champaign, IL: Human Kinetics.

Collins, J. W., Nelson, A., & Sublet, V. (2006). *Safe lifting and nursing home residents.* Cincinnati, Ohio: NIOSH-Publications Dissemination.

Collins, J. W., Wolf, L., Bell, J., & Evanoff, B. (2004). An evaluation of a best practices musculoskeletal injury prevention program in nursing homes. *Injury Prevention, 10*(4), 206-211.

Cromie, J. E., Robertson, J. E., & Best, M. O. (2002). Work-related musculoskeletal disorders and the culture of physical therapy. *Physical Therapy, 82,* 459-472.

Cromie, J. E., Robertson, V. J., & Best, M. O. (2000). Work-related musculoskeletal disorders in physical therapists: prevalence, severity, risks, and responses. *Physical Therapy, 80,* 336-351.

Delisle, A., Lariviere, C., Plamondon, A., & Imbeau, D. (2006). Comparison of three computer office workstations offering forearm support: Impact on upper limb posture and muscle activation. *Ergonomics, 49*(2), 139-160.

Garg, A., & Hegmann, K. (2006). *Applied ergonomics: Low back.* Milwaukee, WI: University of Wisconsin,Milwaukee.

Grandy, M. S., & Westwood, D. A. (2006). Opposite perceptual and sensorimotor Responses to a size-weight illusion. *Journal of Neurophysiology*, 95, 3887-3892.

John, D., Lyden, K., & Bassett, D. (July 2015) A physiological perspective on treadmill and sit-to-stand workstations. Erg.sagepub.com DOI: 10.1177/1064804615585411. Human Factors and Ergonomics Society, July 21, 2015

Keller, S. (2009). Effects of extended work shifts and shift work on patient safety, productivity, and employee health. *American Association of Occupational Health Nurses Journal, 57*(12), 497-502.

Loffler, D., Wallmann-Sperlich, B., Wan, J., Knott, J., Vogel, A., & Hurtienne, J. (July, 2015). Office ergonomics driven by contextual design. Ergonomics in Design. Erg.sagepub.com DOI: 10.1177/1064804615585409. Human Factors and Ergonomics Society, July 21, 2015

Luttmann, A., Jager, M., & Griefahn, B. (n.d.). *Protecting workers' health series no. 5: Preventing musculoskeletal disorders in the workplace.* World Health Organization. Retrieved September 2012, from http://www.who.int/occupational_health/publications/muscdisorders/en/index.html

Marras, W. S., Davis, K. G., Kirking, B. C., & Bertsche, P. K. (1999). A comprehensive analysis of low-back disorder risk and spinal loading during the transferring and repositioning of patients using different techniques. *Ergonomics*, 42(7), 904-926.

Naylor, Y. K., & Amazeen, E. L. (2004). The size-weight illusion in team lifting. *Human Factors: The Journal of the Human Factors and Ergonomics Society*, 46, 349-356.

Nelso, A., Matz, M., Chen, F., Siddarthan, K., Lloyd, J., & Fragala, G. (2006). Development and evaluation of a multifaceted ergonomics program to prevent injuries associated with patient handling tasks. *International Journal of Nursing Studies*, 43, 717-733.

NIOSH. (2007, April 27). Nonfatal occupational injuries and illnesses -- United States 2004. MMWR Weekly. Retrieved August 2012, from http://www.cdc.gov/mmwr/preview/mmwrhtml/mm5616a3.htm

Ogden, C. L., Carroll, M. D., Kit, B. K., & Flegal, K. M. (2012). *Prevalence of obesity in the United States, 2009-1010. NCHS data brief, no 82.* Hyattsville, MD: National Center for Health Statistics.

Pronk, N.P. (July, 2015). Design recommendations for active workplaces. Ergonomics in Design. Erg.sagepub.com DOI: 10.1177/1064804615585408. Human Factors and Ergonomics Society, July 21, 2015

Ramazzini, B. (1940). Diseases of workers (Latin) (W. C. Wright, Trans.). Chicago, IL: University of Chicago Press. (Original work published 1700) found quoted in Pronk, N.P. (July, 2015). Design recommendations for active workplaces. Ergonomics in Design. Erg.sagepub.com DOI: 10.1177/1064804615585408. Human Factors and Ergonomics Society, July 21, 2015

Ripat, J., Scatliff, T., Giesbrect, E., Quanbury, A., Friesen, M., & Kelso, S. (2006). The effect of alternate style keyboards on severity of symptoms and functional status of individuals with work related upper extremity disorders. *Journal of Occupational Rehabilitation*, 16, 707-718.

Sanders, M. S., & McCormick, E. J. (1976). *Human Factors in Engineering and Design* (7th ed.). New York: McGraw-Hill, Inc.

Thomsen, J. F., Gerr, F., & Atroshi, I. (2008). Carpal tunnel syndrome and the use of computer mouse and keyboard: A systematic review. *BMC Musculoskeletal Disorders*, 9(Retrieved from http://www.biomedcentral.com/1471-2474/9/134).

Thornton, A. (2011). Sleep apnea: What employers should know. The American Sleep Apnea Association. Retrieved 2012, from http://www.sleepapnea.org/asaa-blog/sleep-apnea-what-every-employer-should-know.html

US Department of Labor. (2004). OSHA forms for recording work-related injuries and illnesses. Retrieved 2012, from http://www.osha.gov/recordkeeping/new-osha300form1-1-04.pdf

Waersted, M., Hanvold, T. N., & Veiersted, K. B. (2010). *Computer work and musculoskeletal disorders of the neck and upper extremity:* A systematic review. BMC *Musculoskeletal Disorders*, 11(79), 1471-2474.

Woodson, W. E., Tillman, B., & Tillman, P. (1992). *Human factors design handbook* (2nd ed.). New York: McGraw-Hill, Inc.

www.ingramcontent.com/pod-product-compliance
Lightning Source LLC
Chambersburg PA
CBHW080547220326
41599CB00032B/6391